Michael B. Druxman

PAUL MUNI
His Life and His Films

PAUL MUN

His Life and His Films

Michael B. Druxman

SOUTH BRUNSWICK AND NEW YORK: A. S. BARNES AND COMPANY
LONDON: THOMAS YOSELOFF LTD

A. S. Barnes and Co., Inc.
Cranbury, New Jersey 08512

Thomas Yoseloff Ltd
108 New Bond Street
London W1Y OQX, England

Library of Congress Cataloging in Publication Data

Druxman, Michael B 1941–
Paul Muni; his life and his films.

1. Muni, Paul, 1895–1967.
PN2287.M79D7 791.43′028′0924 [B] 73-10519
ISBN 0-498-01413-4

PRINTED IN THE UNITED STATES OF AMERICA

In memory of my father—
Harry Druxman

CONTENTS

Paul Muni and director Mervyn LeRoy on location for *I Am a Fugitive from a Chain Gang.*

FOREWORD

P. M.—I've been thinking of those initials for a long time and I've finally come to the conclusion that they mean *Paul Muni* . . . and, to me, they also mean perfect man . . . perfect actor . . . a real pro.

Having directed this great artist, who, believe me, *was* a great artist, I can only compare him to such other greats in show business and motion pictures as George Arliss, Emil Jannings, Spencer Tracy, David Warfield, James K. Hackett, Fredric March, Jean Gabin, and many others that I can't think of.

I first met Paul Muni when he was doing *Counsellor-at-Law* in New York. In fact, that's the first time I ever saw him. And believe me, greatness stands out.

Paul Muni was a perfectionist. Nothing was good enough for him. He was also a great worrier. Many people have asked me if he was tough to work with. I guess he was one of the *easiest* actors to work with, because he knew his job and did it well.

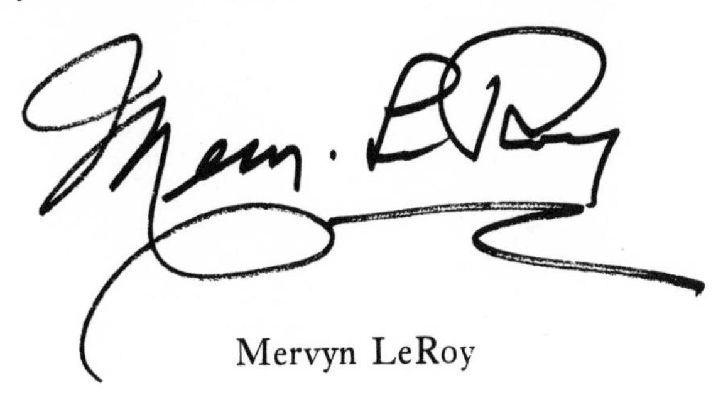

Mervyn LeRoy

ACKNOWLEDGMENTS

Grateful acknowledgment is made to the many individuals and organizations who gave of their time, their knowledge, and/or helped gather stills in the preparation of this book:

Academy of Motion Picture Arts and Sciences, Luther Adler, Vince Barnett, Anne Baxter, Henry Blanke, Eddie Brandt, James Broadhead, Budget Films, Celebrity Service, Marguerite Chapman, Marguerite Churchill, Columbia Pictures, Marc Daniels, Jane Bryan Dart, Luther Davis, Arthur Dreifuss, Douglass Dumbrille, Sidney Ellis, Rudy Fehr, Nina Foch, Glenn Ford, William Gargan, Sheridan Gibney, Sam Jaffe, Allen Jenkins, Jonathan Kidd, Larry Edmunds Bookshop, Jerome Lawrence, Kenneth G. Lawrence, Marc Lawrence, Robert E. Lee, Mervyn LeRoy, Bethel Leslie, Albert Lewis, Milton Lewis, Robert Lieb, Sidney Linden, Karl Malden, Clifford McCarty, Memory Shop, Metro-Goldwyn-Mayer, Arthur Miller, Movie Star News, Paul Myers of the New York Public Library, George O'Brien, Larry Parks, George Raft, RKO Radio Pictures, Harold Rose, Al Rosen, Cosmo Sardo, Selma Soccorso, Ted Thomas, Twentieth-Century Fox, United Artists, Wayne Warga, Warner Brothers, Mr. and Mrs. Joseph Weisenfreund, Cornel Wilde, and Billy Dee Williams.

PAUL MUNI
His Life and His Films

1
THE STAR

Paul Muni was known in the trade as a "prestige" actor, a common euphemism for a star who is not big box-office.

During the 1930s and 40s, "stars" were expected to draw audiences on their names alone, no matter how bad the picture. The name of Gable, Bogart, Cagney, Crawford, Astaire/Rogers, or even Abbott and Costello on a marquee was insurance to the studios that its investment was sound.

Muni was different. True, films like *Zola, The Good Earth,* and *I Am a Fugitive from a Chain Gang* reaped in large grosses, but these were excellent motion pictures in themselves with stories that appealed to the general public. His less successful efforts like *Juarez,* which had major script problems, and the depressing, but excellent, *We Are Not Alone,* were not saved by his presence.

Muni's amazing talent and versatility resulted in his being ranked as one of the truly great actors of this century. He was nominated five times for the Academy Award and won that coveted honor once. He was respected and admired by almost every actor and director who ever worked with him, and has served as the inspiration for countless young actors over the past four decades.

Why, then, did Muni never gain a popular following with the greatest critic of all . . . the public?

The probable answer lies in the very quality that makes him unique

. . . his versatility. Muni never repeated a character. He submerged himself so deeply into his roles that he left none of himself for the audience to identify with.

In contrast, performers like Tracy, Robinson, and Bogart were excellent actors, but no matter how foreign their parts were to them, a bit of their own personalities remained. They adapted the character to themselves, whereas Muni adapted himself to the character.

Viewers may have admired him as James Allen in *Fugitive,* as Louis Pasteur, or as Wang Lung in *The Good Earth,* but each succeeding film had to stand on its own merits. The moviegoer would see a

new character in every picture, and he was, therefore, unable to transfer any charisma to these subsequent projects.

It is doubtful that the average person under thirty today has even heard of Paul Muni. On the other hand, most serious actors, movie buffs, film historians, as well as the "older" generation, consider Muni to be one of, if not *the,* greatest character actor of the last fifty years.

Perhaps, with the current trend toward film nostalgia, the public will rediscover "the man who was always somebody else" and finally give him his just due.

2
THE ACTOR

Paul Muni never attended an acting school, nor did he ever read a book on the subject. He didn't trust systems and theories of the craft, because he felt it couldn't be analyzed to any great extent.

He once said in an interview: "The last thing I want to think about is *how* I achieve an effect."

In its obituary of Muni, *Newsweek* referred to the performer as "the greatest character actor of his day."

Actor Douglass Dumbrille, who appeared in three early pictures with him, calls Muni "the most dedicated actor I have ever known."

For the most part, the actors and actresses that worked with Muni considered it a privilege and echo Dumbrille's sentiments. He was the "ideal" . . . almost a legend. Nobody was as good as Muni. Those that were lucky enough to do a play or film with him consider it an experience they will never forget.

One of the few negative notes comes from Marguerite Churchill, the actor's leading lady in his first two films, *The Valiant* and *Seven Faces*. She found him "boring."

The basis of Muni's naturalistic technique was *research*. Everything stemmed from that. When he played a character from history, such as Zola, Pasteur, or Clarence Darrow, he would read everything available on the person, as well as their contemporaries. He'd study photographs, documents, and, whenever possible, visit the places where the subject lived.

In playing a fictional character, the method was no different. For *Black Fury,* he spent several weeks in an Eastern coal town. *I Am a Fugitive from a Chain Gang* found him visiting prisons, and, prior to the filming of *The Good Earth,* he haunted San Francisco's Chinatown for several months.

The Good Earth.

The Good Earth was two weeks into principal photography when producer Irving Thalberg phoned Mervyn LeRoy to ask a favor. LeRoy had previously directed Muni in three films, including *Chain Gang.*

"I'd like you to call Muni and explain something to him," requested the young producer.

"What's the problem?" asked LeRoy.

"Tell Muni that I want him to be a Chinaman in the picture . . . but not a *real* Chinaman."

Thalberg was only half in jest. He had never worked with the actor before and found it somewhat disconcerting that he would remain in character, even when he was not before the cameras.

According to Luther Adler, "Muni never took himself seriously . . . only his work."

Muni perfected his craft in the practical school, where actors learned by acting. He seldom talked about his technique. However, in 1940, while doing *Key Largo* on Broadway, he granted an interview to Morton Eustis of *Theatre Arts,* in which he discussed his methods:

"If I were to use a principle at all in acting, it would be that if the mind—the basic generator—functions alertly and sums up its impulses and conclusions to a correct result, it is possible for the actor to achieve something creative. Technique, which comes with practice, gives you the firm foundation on which to build your structure. But unless the mind sends out the sparks, the forces that stimulate the body to perform a series of actions that generate a spontaneous emotion, nothing creative can happen.

"If his [the actor's] apparatus up here [in the brain] is not functioning, all the technique in the world won't save him; if it is, I'd almost say that the technique would take care of itself."

When he was not in a serious mood, Muni would compare his theory of acting to his wife's grandmother's method of making apple pie. When she was asked the secret of how she made such delicious pies, she would reply: "First, I comb my hair. Then I wash my hands. Then I put on my apron. Then I make apple pie."

Muni discussed other aspects of his technique with the writer from *Theatre Arts:* "I never think, in reading a script, that I will use such and such a gesture here, or that this is the point at which effect number twenty-two should be pulled out of the hat. If I were consciously to do certain things to attain certain effects, I'd become self-conscious and lose the ability to create a spontaneous impression."

Whereas he may not have assigned his character a specific action on a particular line during the *early* stages of his preparation for a role, by the time Muni went before the cameras or walked on stage in front of an audience, that characterization was ninety-nine percent set and almost totally inflexible.

Muni would insist on getting his scripts months in advance, in order to help facilitate his research and allow him time to absorb the material until it became "a part of him."

On the set for *Juarez.*

The actor would read every role into a dictaphone or tape recorder, then play it back so that he could learn his lines, perfect his dialect, and check interpretation, as well as anticipate the possible interpretations of his fellow performers. On occasion, to get the physical aspects of his character correct, he would work in front of a mirror. Finally, he would "closet" himself in his study for days, experimenting with various makeups. In a stage production, his makeup would change almost every night of tryouts until he achieved the desired effect.

When Muni's character was where *he* wanted it to be, it was virtually impossible to get him to make a change of any sort.

During the filming of *Juarez,* director William Dieterle told the actor to make his entrance in a particular scene from stage left. Muni objected: "I can't do that," he explained. "I *set* the scene at home so that I come in stage right."

There was much discussion on the issue, with associate producer Henry Blanke being brought in to settle the matter. It was decided that, since such an adjustment would upset the star to the point where it might impair his performance, another solution must be found. Eventually, Blanke ordered the entire set in question rebuilt to go along with Muni's demand that he enter stage right. In addition, several scenes had to be refilmed so the editor would be able to "match" the direction in which Muni was moving in those shots with the revamped scene.

On later films, such as *A Song to Remember* and *Angel on My Shoulder,* when he was no longer in as powerful a position as he was at Warner Brothers and was *forced* to *adjust* to the director's requirements, Muni would, according to observers, go into a temper tantrum and much time would pass before he would settle down.

Once they master their lines, most actors predetermine what they will actually do during performance in only the most general terms, choosing instead to "play the moment." Few have the ability to choreograph a role in detail, such as Muni would do, and make it look anything except "mechanical."

But Muni still retained the *ability to listen* to other actors, then *react* to what they were saying, rather than just employ effect number twenty-two at a given point. The entire performance may have been preplanned, right down to that proverbial effect number twenty-two, but, in Muni's hands, it came across as being completely fresh.

The actor would always hear out his director, however would seldom be helped by his suggestions, preferring to develop his characterization within himself . . . generally to the point where he would lose his own identity.

With director William Dieterle and Bella on the set of *Juarez.*

Muni, always the perfectionist, was extremely selective in the scripts he chose to do. His entire film career consisted of twenty-three pictures. He did eleven shows on Broadway, one of which was a revival of his earlier success, *Counsellor-at-Law.* In addition, he starred in the London company of *Death of a Salesman* and opened in two other stage productions, which never reached New York. Lastly, there were five *significant* television appearances.

A close associate of Jack L. Warner feels that Muni "tried too hard for an ideal that just wasn't there. He would never repeat a role and, during his last few years at Warners, insisted that every script be the quality of *Zola*."

Muni never accepted a role strictly for the money . . . even at the start of his film career, when he refused to sign a contract with William Fox until it was specified what his first project would be. He always looked for a script that, aside from having a role for him to play that was "vital and lifelike," was also in good taste and had something to say. There may have been some poor choices and/or unfortunate results along the way, but, at least at their conception, Muni believed in the project.

He didn't like to be repetitive in his roles. After *Scarface* was released, the actor, who was then on tour with *Counsellor-at-Law,* received a wire from Cecil B. DeMille offering him a role "just like *Scarface*." Muni wired back: "I've already done *Scarface*. Not interested."

Muni was never totally satisfied with any of his films. He felt that he was "conned" into doing many of the projects with promises that were seldom kept. As he told Luther Adler: "They kissed my ass to get me to do *The Last Angry Man*."

His inexperience with the filmmaking process caused him great emotional stress during his early days in Hollywood. Actor George O'Brien, who was under contract to Fox at the same time as Muni, recalls an incident: "Muni and I became very friendly at the studio. He was a fan of mine from *Sunrise,* which I had done a couple of years before.

"We attended the sneak preview of *Seven Faces* together at the Criterion Theatre in Santa Monica. He was so upset with the way they had cut the picture, that, after the screening, he burst into tears. We walked along the beach for a couple of hours, while I quieted him down by explaining the pitfalls of the industry."

Muni never really enjoyed making movies. Directors on his pictures learned quickly not to tell their star if they were planning a long shot or a close-up. The actor didn't want to be *that* aware of the camera or the other technical aspects of the art, since he thought they should have no significant effect on his ultimate performance.

He seldom would hold up shooting and, then, only if his instinct, which was almost always right, told him there was something seriously wrong with a scene. When *Counter-Attack* was before the cameras, he stopped production for a full day because he felt that a particular prop was being used incorrectly.

The actor's severest critic was his wife, Bella. When it came to his performances, he trusted her opinion implicitly. She was almost always on the set or at the theater during rehearsals. She would stand behind the director and, when Muni finished a scene or a take, he'd look at her. If she nodded, he knew his performance was fine. But if she shook her head, he asked to do it again, even if the director was satisfied. Muni was not at his best when Bella wasn't around. Such a

Publicity shot from *At the Grand.*

case was *A Song to Remember.* In that instance, Harry Cohn, head of Columbia Pictures, had her barred from the set. It was Muni's poorest performance on film.

All scripts sent to Muni were read by Bella first. If she thought they had merit, she'd pass them on to her husband. She was usually correct in her judgment. But, at times, she made mistakes. She suggested that he refuse *High Sierra* (eventually filmed with Humphrey Bogart) because it would be another gangster role and she didn't want him "typed" in that sort of part. Some insist that Muni was the initial choice for Arthur Miller's *Death of a Salesman* on Broadway, but Bella, not impressed with the script, talked him out of it.

For the most part, while he was on a set, Muni was unapproachable, wanting to remain "in character" as much as possible. Bella "protected" him from cast and crew members that might wish to talk with him, politely informing the inquirer: "Mr. Muni does not communicate with anyone." She would bring his food to his dressing room and, between takes, cue him on his lines.

When he did a stage play, other actors were advised not to speak to Muni after he left his dressing room to make his first entrance of the evening. During a performance of *Inherit the Wind,* an uninformed extra stopped the star when he was about to go on stage. "Mr. Muni," exclaimed the excited youth, "Harry Truman is in the audience!"

"I don't give a shit!" retorted Muni, as he made his entrance.

Soon after he came to Warner Brothers, Muni arranged for the studio to hire Abem Finkel, Bella's brother, as a writer. Whenever Muni was unhappy with a script, he would insist that Finkel "doctor" it because the writer knew "what *he* wanted."

Unfortunately for Finkel, who was, in fact, a talented man, he became known around the lot as "Muni's writer" and some of the other writers resented him. Aside from doing films for Muni, such as *Black Fury* and *Hi, Nellie,* he collaborated on other pictures, including *Jezebel, Marked Woman, Black Legion,* and *Sergeant York.*

Although they were seldom obvious to an audience, Muni had two major problems as an actor . . . both of which stemmed from his early years with the Yiddish Theatre.

Actors on the Yiddish stage played their roles in very broad terms, incorporating exaggerated emotions and gestures. Muni carried this "tendency to ham" with him when he entered the English-speaking theatre and, later, films. In most cases, he was able to keep the problem under control. But when Bella was not around to guide him or he was working with a "weak" director, as were the cases with *Hudson's Bay* and *A Song to Remember,* he would slip back into the Yiddish technique with an unfortunate result.

Whenever an interviewer asked Spencer Tracy to give out with some words of wisdom for young actors, Spence's immediate answer would be, "Learn your lines." The Yiddish Theatre didn't follow this philosophy and relied heavily on prompters. The actors never bothered to learn their roles as thoroughly as they otherwise might have. They had the security of knowing that, should they go "blank" during the performance, there was somebody there to get them back on the track.

Because he never developed a technique for memorizing his dialogue, Muni always had trouble in this area after he left the Yiddish stage. It was one of the reasons that he always insisted on getting his scripts months in advance . . . so he could record his lines on a dictaphone and play them back until he had them down exactly. He would still have problems with long speeches and would often require several takes to get them correct.

Bethel Leslie, who was in *Inherit the Wind,* reports that he insisted on a "running prompt" during the first few weeks of performance. In fact, the first night of tryouts, he didn't seem to know a line. However, his performance didn't suffer and, as she recalls, he was "brilliant in Philadelphia."

Robert Lieb, appearing in the same play, was forced to "throw Muni a line" on stage one night when the actor went "blank." But, as soon as he caught the "key word," he was right back on the track.

Muni always arrived at the theater very early, so that he could apply his makeup and slip into character. He would remain "in character" until the end of the evening's performance.

One thing could "throw" Muni on stage . . . the color *red.* It had an unexplained psychological effect on him and could be responsible for his breaking concentration. James Broadhead, an extra in *Wind,* unknowingly wore red socks in a performance one night and was almost fired after the curtain came down.

Muni would never allow people to watch him from the wings, since this also could distract him. Karl Malden recalls that, during performances of *Key Largo,* the star would actually yell at observers to move away from his line of vision.

When he was doing the 1942 revival of *Counsellor-at-Law,* actor Jonathan Kidd (AKA Kurt Richards) asked permission to watch Muni play a highly dramatic telephone scene. Replied the star: "Are they going to replace me?"

"Of course not," laughed Kidd. "I just thought I might learn something."

"You're an optimist."

Kidd was granted permission, as long as he didn't let Muni see him.

Once he got a role down pat, Muni would not be above ad-libbing on stage . . . sometimes in order to "put down" another actor who might be getting out of line.

Bob Lieb recalls an incident from *Inherit the Wind,* which illustrates the point: "There was a young actor, who had done a few fairly good roles on Broadway in past seasons. Unfortunately, he had had a couple of lean months and, in order to pay the rent, took a job as an extra in the play. Having to 'lower' himself to extra status really ate at this guy's ego and he became pretty resentful.

"The play was based on the Scopes 'Monkey' trial and its most important scene was the one where Muni, as Clarence Darrow, puts Ed Begley, playing William Jennings Bryan, on the witness stand to testify as an expert on the Bible. At one point in the interrogation, Begley says something profound, the courtroom spectators shout 'Amen,' and Muni retorts with 'I want those "Amen's" on the record!'

"This actor we're talking about used to vent his frustration by coming in every night with *his* 'Amen' a beat or two after the other extras. This would rile Muni, but, as his back was to the spectators at that point, he couldn't pinpoint the guilty party.

"In one performance, this dunce slipped up and came in with a long 'Amen' on Muni's line. Muni spotted him and pointed his finger right at the performer, while saying: 'I want those "Amens" on the record . . . especially that one over there, who *won't* be there tomorrow night!'

"And he wasn't there the next night."

In 1931, the late John Anderson discussed Muni's talent in an issue of *Theatre Arts:* "Muni knows how to make every moment in a performance count and is willing to take his time in doing it. He leaves no blurred edges, nor any frayed outlines. They are sharp, clear, in full focus because he sees them himself, and commands the fluency and vitality to show what he is thinking about. There is power and richness of texture in his acting, and a sort of personal violence that is carefully used for touches that are compelling and unforgettable."

In other words . . . he was a *damned good* actor.

3
THE MAN

He was a very private man. Nobody, with the possible exception of his wife, really knew him. Friends, relatives, and associates only saw the sides of his personality he wanted to expose. He was an enigma.

Actor Luther Adler claims that anybody who says they were close to Paul Muni is a "liar."

Jane Bryan played opposite him in *We Are Not Alone* and describes the artist as being "many people rolled into one."

A cousin, writer Sid Ellis, reflects that it was often difficult to look Muni straight in the eye. There was a sadnesss there . . . a sense of loss, which made one uneasy.

"He was a lonely man," says actor/director Marc Lawrence, "because art is a lonely business."

His last agent, Harold Rose, remembers Muni as the most "unique" client he ever represented—truly, "a rugged individualist."

Jonathan Kidd (AKA Kurt Richards) was in the 1942 revival of *Counsellor-at-Law:* "Muni had a 'childlike wonder' about him, which was unusual in a mature man."

Karl Malden worked in the Broadway version of *Key Largo* and describes the actor as "a man in his midforties, who moved like he was eighty."

Bethel Leslie, a good friend during his last years, had appeared

Publicity shot.

with Muni in *Inherit the Wind:* "I remember the great intensity of the man. Yet, he had a wry, pixieish humor. If he liked you, he could keep you laughing for hours with stories and jokes from the Yiddish Theatre."

The most important influence in Muni's life was Bella, his wife. She was his "buffer." She fought his battles and shielded him from the outside world. Handling the family finances was also her responsibility and she did an excellent job of it, investing heavily in blue-chip stocks.

Yet, according to those that knew them, there was no "mad love affair" between the two. It was a convenient marriage, almost a partnership. Bella's keen business and artistic sense was a great help to Muni. It freed him to concentrate on what interested him most . . . his art. She, in turn, achieved a status by marrying him that she would probably never have gained otherwise.

It was a good match. They liked one another and, over the years, this feeling turned into affection. Neither one wanted children. They were just two close companions, who, if nothing else, needed each other.

Muni's brother, Joseph Weisenfreund, recalls a time in the early forties when the actor confided to him that Bella was spending too much money redecorating their house. He had recently terminated his contract with Warner Brothers and no longer had a steady income.

"Why don't you complain?" asked Joe.

"I don't want to hurt her feelings," was the reply.

Muni had a fear of poverty that stemmed from his childhood, when his impoverished family was forced to live with various friends, relatives, and strangers. In his adult life, he never relied on credit, paying *cash* for everything . . . even his homes. He never wanted to be placed in a position where a bank or other creditor could repossess anything he owned.

Although he only bought land to live on and never as an investment, Muni would often make a considerable profit when he went to sell his home. Strangely enough, he didn't care about making money on the property and, for the most part, only asked for the land what he paid for it.

He was a millionaire at the time of his death, yet the actor was

Muni writes a "ticket" for a motor officer, while director Mervyn LeRoy looks on. Gag photo taken for *I Am a Fugitive.*

quite the "penny-pincher" . . . sometimes to the point of being foolish. He seldom took cabs, relying on the bus or subway to take him to the theater or to an airport. When he received the physician's bill for his eye operation, he "screamed" that the fee was "outrageous," oblivious of the fact that the surgery had probably saved his life.

On the other hand, there were times when he could be very generous. He supported his mother for years and, when he became successful in Hollywood, he purchased and deeded two houses in the San Fernando Valley to his brothers. A few years later, he paid off a second mortgage brother Joe had incurred on his home. Joe was unaware that the note had been paid until *after* the deed was done.

Muni had no use for distant relatives located in various parts of the country, even though they might be able to supply him with information about his family's beginnings in Europe. He felt that they would only "want something" from him.

However, when Hitler was persecuting the Jews in the midthirties, Muni sent several thousand dollars to relatives in Leipzig, so they could escape to Israel.

He could be generous with strangers. In 1947, he did a summer stock production of *Counsellor-at-Law* at the Marble Head Playhouse in Marble Head, Massachusetts. His contract with the theater gave him a guaranteed salary against a percentage of the gross receipts. The actor kept the basic salary, but insisted that the cast get the percentage, to be divided in inverse proportion to the importance of their roles. In other words, the actors with the smallest parts received the largest bonus and vice versa.

Muni was very gracious to the "secondary" people who worked with him. He always had a friendly greeting for the other actors and extras, as well as the stage hands, and would often take a few minutes to chat with them about various topics. He enjoyed talking with people that he liked.

When he *was* with somebody he liked, Muni might step completely out of character. Karl Malden remembers that he was always being surprised by Muni. "We were in Washington D.C. doing *Key Largo.* One afternoon, Muni and I were leaving the theater to get a bite to eat. I'd always considered him rather a serious man, so I was taken aback when he ran out into the street and halted traffic. Afterwards, he said: 'I bet you never thought I could do that.' "

Sometimes he would take a personal interest in a performer. During the filming of *A Song to Remember,* he called Nina Foch into his dressing room and asked her, quite bluntly, "Do you want to be a good actress or a professional whore?"

Recalls Miss Foch: "In his own way, he was telling me that I could continue working in films and learn nothing or continue to study my craft and become an accomplished performer. The talk had a profound effect on my life and career.

"Muni was a lovely man. I'm sorry I wasn't able to work with him again when I could appreciate it."

With Bella on an evening out (1939).

Most actors have their feelings of inferiority and fears of failure. Muni was no exception. He never considered himself to be an attractive man, which, according to his brother Joe, was part of the reason he married Bella. She was the only woman that was attracted to him.

His psychological problems manifested themselves in his becoming a recluse. He seldom went to Hollywood parties, premieres, or other functions, choosing to go right home after finishing work at the studio. He had few friends.

When he was not involved with a film or stage production, he would spend his time listening to music or reading. He allegedly owned 450 dictionaries . . . in every conceivable language.

He was a "gadget fiend." He could never pass a stationery store without going in to see if there was a new type of pen or paper clip on the market.

Tape recorders were another passion. He owned approximately a dozen of them and they were constantly in use to help him develop his characterizations, learn dialogue, record interesting passages from a book he might be reading, or to conduct business.

Agent Harold Rose recalls an incident that occurred while the deal for *The Last Angry Man* was being negotiated: "The first draft of the contracts were sent over for Muni's approval. He must have gone over them with a magnifying glass, checking every comma. He showed up at my office the next day for a meeting with the attorney from the studio . . . carrying two tape recorders. The three of us sat there for two and one-half hours listening to the detailed changes Muni wanted in the agreement . . . all of which were recorded on tape. The lawyer tried to object once, but Muni cut him off with 'I don't care what you've done before. This is the way *I* do it!' "

He had an aversion to tardiness. If invited dinner guests did not arrive at his home exactly on time, Muni and Bella would begin eating without them. His explanation: "If a man steals money or property from you, that's one thing. But, if he steals time, he steals a piece of your life."

Muni did not care for Christmas. Often, Bella would spend the holiday with friends, while Muni stayed at home by himself. In fact, the couple spent considerable time apart. Bella would go to the theater or concerts by herself and Muni would even go on European vacations alone.

Although he didn't practice his religion, Muni was a proud Jew and hated anti-Semitism. Once, during a play rehearsal, he punched an actor who had made a nasty remark.

He liked to tell Yiddish jokes and would josh with people in that

On the set of *Juarez:* Monte Blue (left) receives a birthday cake from Muni and director William Dieterle.

language. Sid Ellis recalls a time that Muni was caught in traffic on the way to the Hollywood Bowl. In the car across from him was James Cagney . . . in the same predicament. When the two spotted each other, they laughed, then began shouting Yiddish insults back and forth.

The actor liked dogs and always had at least one. He also enjoyed driving a car, prize fights, shooting galleries, and checkers.

Muni never took too much care in how he dressed. One friend described him as looking "like he just got off the boat from Europe." He seldom paid attention to superficial things, such as his outward appearance, and never thought it important to have clothing in the *latest* style.

However, he was still human. When he did *Inherit the Wind* in New York, Edward G. Robinson was starring at the same time on Broadway in *Middle of the Night.* One Sunday, Muni attended a benefit performance of Robinson's play and, after the show, visited his old friend backstage.

At home during the mid-1940s with Bella and dog Toto.

Robert P. Lieb, a member of the *Wind* cast, recalls that, "the following evening, Muni could only talk about Robinson's elegantly decorated dressing room, his Park Avenue apartment and chauffeured limousine, which brought him to the theater every night. 'I remember when he was a spear-carrier,' he would say. Muni was so impressed, he went out and hired himself a chauffeured limousine . . . the most expensive available. He wasn't going to be bested.

"What he didn't realize was that Robinson had all these luxuries written into his contract and the producers were paying for them."

Muni was not one to go out and publicize his films or plays. When he was trying out *Inherit the Wind* in Philadelphia, the owner of the theater asked him to do a local radio show. He refused, claiming, "I don't do radio for money. Why should I do it free?"

"But it will make more money for the show," was the reply.

"I'm an actor," he retorted. "I'm not in the money-making business."

Nevertheless, he was always ready to protect his financial interest. Part of his deal for the revival of *Counsellor-at-Law* in 1942 included a percentage of the gross receipts. The actor learned that the management was giving out two-for-one passes (patron pays for one ticket and gets the second free) in order to fill the theater on slow nights, and his temper exploded. He stormed into the manager's office, yelling and screaming. The practice was stopped.

Muni was a man of his word and expected the people he dealt with to follow his example. To him, a bargain was a bargain. He refused to film scenes from *The Last Angry Man* until script changes he was guaranteed by the producer, *prior* to his signing the contract, were made. Years before, he had torn up his lucrative Warner Brothers contract because he felt that the men in power had broken their promises to him.

He hated the sham and pretentiousness that was and is a natural part of the entertainment industry, and avoided it as much as he could. He insisted on being "his own man."

Muni felt that film producers had a responsibility to the public and he aired this view on several occasions. In 1938, he said in a newspaper interview: "Do you know that gangsters really emulated the ones that we created on the screen?—trying to be 'Little Caesars' and 'Scarfaces!' Kids, too.

"That's bad. Today the newspapers share with pictures the responsibility of disseminating knowledge that will do the most good. People believe what they see—and I'm not speaking only of the moron level either. 'Steering the ship' will take plenty of work in the near future!"

According to Sid Ellis, "If one were to sum up what Muni wanted out of life, it would probably boil down to three things: beauty, privacy, and accessibility to work."

The man *was* a puzzle. Perhaps, if all the pieces are ever put together, Ellis's simple description might be correct.

Perhaps.

4
THE CAREER

People called him *Muni* . . . not *Paul* . . . not *Mr. Muni* . . . just *Muni*. It was the name his parents had given him and, although he'd changed it legally, he felt uncomfortable being addressed any other way.

Muni Weisenfreund was born on September 22, 1895 in Lemberg, Austria, which is now part of Poland. He was the youngest of three sons born to Nathan Philip and Sally Weisenfreund, who were strolling players in the ghettos of Eastern Europe. Their repertoire consisted of songs, dances, and dramatic sketches, and they traveled from town to town by horse and carriage, performing in barns.

Sally Weisenfreund, whose maiden name was Fischler, came from a wealthy Jewish family. However, when she married an actor (the profession, in those days, was not highly regarded), her father was furious and disowned her. At his death, all his money went to "strangers."

The life of a strolling performer in Europe was not one of abundance. The Weisenfreunds would be forced to live for a night or two with strangers, then move on. Their food, literally, consisted of leftovers. Also, anti-Semitic feelings on the Continent ran high.

Mrs. Weisenfreund's two step-brothers lived in New York City. One was a peddler and the other owned a restaurant. Having this

The Weisenfreund family: Ellis (with hoop), Nathan, Muni (on lap), Sally, and Joseph. Taken in 1896 in Austria.

The Weisenfreund brothers: Ellis, Muni, and Joseph. Taken in 1898.

"family" tie with the United States, the Weisenfreunds decided to work their way over to the "land of opportunity."

The couple, with sons Joseph, Ellis, and Muni in tow, eventually got to London, where Nathan rented a theater in the White Chapel district. Here, in the ghetto area, he and Sally performed Yiddish vaudeville. They did well for a time until, one evening, a gang fight broke out on the steps of the theater. A man was killed and Nathan, subsequently, testified at a murder trial.

Following the incident, the theater box-office suffered and Nathan was forced to close down. But the Weisenfreunds had already accomplished their aim . . . to raise a stake to take them to America.

Nathan crossed the Atlantic first and, after he got a foothold in the new country, sent for his family. They arrived in New York, via steerage, near the end of 1900.

The family moved into a sixth-floor cold-water flat on Clinton Street near the Yiddish theatrical neighborhood. Nathan had assembled a group of performers, including Belle Baker and Sophie Tucker, and they were doing vaudeville at the Clinton Roof Garden.

Muni was enrolled in his first school, P.S. No. 20 at Rivington and Forsythe Streets on the East Side. It was about this time that he had a bout with rheumatic fever and, although he obviously recovered, his health remained fragile for the remainder of his life. In his later years, Muni always enjoyed relating how, at age thirty-six, he was told by a doctor that he had only six months to live.

There was much competition in Yiddish vaudeville and the family's living was meager. However, Nathan managed to save enough for his sons to take violin lessons, envisioning that the three would someday become great concert artists.

In 1905, the family departed New York in hopes that they could improve their fortunes in another city. They eventually wound up in Cleveland, where Joseph was enrolled in musical college and Nathan and Sally became part of the permanent company of a Yiddish theater.

It was in Cleveland that Muni made his first stage appearance at the age of twelve. He had long been interested in going on the stage, but his father had discouraged the idea, wanting his youngest son to study the violin also.

Then, in 1907, one of the actors in the company became ill and Muni, behind a heavy beard and makeup, went on stage as an elderly lodge president in the sketch, *Two Corpses at Breakfast.* He did well and the manager invited him to join the company at ten dollars per week. Since this extra money brought the family's total weekly income up to thirty-five dollars, Nathan agreed to let his son accept the offer.

The Weisenfreund family in 1903: front row—Nathan and Sally; second row—Joseph and Ellis; top—Muni.

So, Muni learned his art in the most practical school—acting itself. In the early years, most of his roles required beards, and the youth found himself portraying everything from a rabbi to a Cossack. He enjoyed playing with makeup and would often spend his spare time working on new effects. One of his favorite creations was his makeup for Mephistopheles, in which he pasted gold paper on his eyelids. When the spotlight was turned on him, "fire" shot from his eyes.

The following year, the Weisenfreunds moved to Chicago, where

During his teens.

As a teenager.

Nathan leased a small theater on 12th Street and produced short plays in Yiddish for the admission price of ten cents. The family was very close during this period, with all members doing their part to help the venture succeed. Muni appeared in virtually every production and, in one instance, played Nathan's father.

Joseph Weisenfreund recalls that, in about 1912, he watched his brother do a Yiddish play, entitled *Barkochba*. "As I sat there, a

As a teenager with his mother.

'tingle' went down my spine. I always knew that Muni was good, but, at that moment, I realized that he had that 'spark of greatness.' "

In 1913, Nathan Weisenfreund died of pleurisy pneumonia. Sally sold the balance of the theater lease and joined a Yiddish touring company. For a short time, Muni sold used clothing. Unsuccessful at that, he joined his mother on the road.

A few years later, Sally Weisenfreund married Morris Nasiter, a prompter with the Yiddish theater, and retired. It was a good marriage and Nasiter, subsequently, became an insurance adjuster. Sally died in 1934.

Muni continued traveling with the troupe throughout the Middle Western states until 1917. He played everything from Ibsen and Strindberg to burlesque . . . all in his native tongue, Yiddish.

Jacob Kalich, husband of Molly Picon and manager of a Boston company, invited the young man to come to that city and join their group. Unfortunately, the company floundered during the influenza epidemic of 1918 and Muni, in order to eat, moved on to Philadelphia to do some vaudeville.

He was about to sign a contract with another legitimate theater, when Maurice Schwartz, the dean of Yiddish actors, saw him work and offered him a place with the Yiddish Art Theatre in New York at forty-five dollars per week. As Muni once described it, "The Yiddish Art Theatre was *the* theatre." Its ranks contained the greatest Yiddish actors of the time, such as: Celia Adler, Mme. Appel, Ludwig Satz, Jacob Ben-Ami, Clara Rosenthal, Boris Rosenthal, and, of course, Schwartz.

Muni remained with Schwartz from 1918 until 1926 and learned a great deal. He toured the United States and England, playing a variety of roles, such as Yivanov in Sholom Aleichem's *Hard to Be a Jew,* David Leizer in Andreev's *Anathema,* Osip in Gogol's *Inspector General,* the father in Gorky's *Middle Class People,* and the aristocrat in Romain Rolland's *Wolves.*

Critics began to notice Muni. The *New York Times* labeled his performance in *Anathema* as "excellent" and the same paper said of *Wolves,* ". . . Maurice Schwartz and Muni Weisenfreund throughout wear the trappings of the Rolland philosophy without ever becoming the mere parrots of his lines."

There is a legend about Muni, of how he would, dressed and made up as an old man with long hair and a flowing beard, terrify the children that played in the alley behind the theater by roller skating past them with wild agility. The actor enjoyed playing such pranks while waiting for his cues.

In the Yiddish Art Theatre production of *The Inspector General.*

In the Yiddish Art Theatre production of *Wolves.*

Bella and Muni shortly after their wedding.

It was during his association with the Yiddish Art Theatre that he met Bella Finkel, a slim, dark-haired beauty, who was a member of the company. Miss Finkel was the niece of Boris Thomashefsky, considered the "John Barrymore" of the Yiddish Theatre, and was, in her own right, a "star."

Bella's background was tragic. Her father, also an actor, had shot her mother in a jealous rage and then taken his own life. The mother, Emma, lived, but was crippled by the attack and spent the remainder of her life in a wheelchair. The violent incident took place in front of the couple's three teenage children.

Muni and Bella were married on May 8, 1921. Immediately after the rabbi completed the ceremony in downtown Manhattan, Muni shook hands with his new bride and hurried off to do a matinee. That evening, after the final performance, he met her at a subway, escorted her home to her mother, and left her there. During the next two weeks, he phoned her regularly. The honeymoon finally began fifteen days later, when the couple went on tour with a show.

Albert Lewis, who co-produced *We Americans* with Sam Harris on Broadway, recalls how Muni finally came to the English-speaking theatre:

"We had originally set Edward G. Robinson to star in *We Americans*. He played the role for two weeks during tryouts, but because of a previous commitment with the Theatre Guild, was forced to withdraw. Sam Harris and I were stuck for a leading man until Edward Relkin, press agent for the Yiddish Art Theatre, suggested we take a look at a young actor named Muni Weisenfreund.

"The play we saw was *It's Hard to Be a Jew* and Muni didn't make his entrance until the last act. He was excellent. After the show, I was surprised that he was such a young man, since the character he was playing was so old."

We Americans by Milton Herbert Gropper and Max Siegel opened on Broadway at the Sam Harris Theatre in October of 1926, under the direction of Sam Forrest. Also in the cast were Luther Adler and Charles Ellis. The comedy dealt with the generation gap in a Jewish family. Muni played the elderly father, Morris Levine.

The production ran for 118 performances. Of the actor, the *New York Times* said: "There is an authentic performance of an old man by an actor named Muni Weisenfreund. . . ."

Other critics commented that it was "sad" that such a fine actor as Weisenfreund had to wait until so late in his career to get an opportunity to appear on Broadway.

Muni was thirty-one years old.

We Americans.

Lewis brought producer John Golden to see the production and, the following season, Golden cast Muni in *Four Walls,* a play by Dana Burnet and George Abbott, which opened at the John Golden Theatre in September of 1927, under Abbott's direction. In the cast were Muni's wife, Bella, Lee Strasberg, William Pawley, and Sanford Meisner.

The play gave Muni the rare opportunity to play a young man.

Four Walls.

He was Benny Horowitz, an ex-convict attempting to "go straight" after his release from Sing Sing, only to land back in prison after he kills the leader of his old gang. Said the *New York Times:* "There is first and foremost, Mr. Weisenfreund, who, playing his second English speaking part, contributes a sensitive, understanding and full-rounded portrayal of an East Side youth who, caught in the vise-like grip of his environment, manages to evolve a set of home-made ideals and remain true to them."

Talking pictures were becoming a reality and Hollywood producers were looking for actors with trained voices. Albert Lewis had become an executive for William Fox Studios and he suggested that Fox and studio production head, Winfield Sheehan, go to New York and take a look at Muni, who was then appearing in the Golden production.

Fox and Sheehan were impressed with the young actor and ordered a screen test. The test was both extensive and expensive. In it, Muni performed scenes from Eugene O'Neill's *The Hairy Ape* and Shakespeare's *The Merry Wives of Windsor.* Again, the producers liked what they saw and signed Muni to a three-year contract, with options, at a starting salary of five hundred dollars per week progressing to fifteen hundred dollars in the third year.

Shortly before they were to leave for Hollywood, Muni and Bella came to Albert Lewis, who had become a good friend, and told him they were having "second thoughts" about the deal.

Recalls Lewis: "Bella insisted that Muni know what scripts he was going to do. She wanted a clause added to the contract that would stipulate what Muni's first film would be. They were afraid that he might go out to Hollywood and get assigned to appear in a western or something else beneath his caliber."

Lewis talked with Sheehan and they came up with the idea of putting Muni in Molnar's *Liliom,* a property then owned by Metro-Goldwyn-Mayer. The actor accepted the idea and Lewis, subsequently, negotiated a deal with Metro to purchase the story.

The Weisenfreunds came to Hollywood and, shortly after their arrival, Sheehan convinced the actor that he should change his name to *Paul Muni.* Initial Fox publicity releases called him a new discovery from Russia.

A poll of theater owners around the country indicated that the exhibitors were not interested in buying *Liliom* with an unknown named Paul Muni in the leading role. The studio temporarily abandoned the project, but later filmed it with Charles Farrell.

Early publicity shot taken by Fox Studios about 1929.

Muni was furious and wanted out of his contract. In order to placate the actor, numerous properties were submitted to him. One script was *The Holy Devil,* a story of Rasputin, which had Raoul Walsh set to direct. He finally chose to do a screen version of a one-act play by Robert Middlemass and Holworthy Hall, entitled *The Valiant.* According to Lewis, "He liked it because he equated it to *Four Walls.*"

Muni was cast as James Dyke, a convicted murderer, who goes to the electric chair, denying his identity, so his family will be spared the humiliation of the crime. Muni received unanimous praise from the critics for this 1929 release and, although the film itself was not successful, it earned the "rookie" his first Academy Award nomination.

The fact that *The Valiant* was such a box-office bomb came as a considerable shock and disappointment to Fox and Sheehan. They decided not to inform Muni of the bad news and, in order to complete their first year's commitment, assigned him to star in *Seven Faces,* based on Richard Connell's *Friend of Napoleon.*

The actor was aware that the screenplay left much to be desired, but Muni liked the idea of the role, which allowed him, in fact, to play seven totally different characters. The publicity campaign on the picture centered around this aspect, calling Muni another Lon Chaney. Needless to say, Muni was not enthusiastic about the comparison.

About the time the picture was released in 1929, Muni gave an interview, in which he discussed makeup: "Some screen actors, who have worked up a tremendous reputation as character men by appearing in different make-up in each picture, have never rung true to me because I can see their personality behind their disguises. Their foundation isn't right. In order to characterize effectively, it is more important to masquerade the mind than the body. It is possible for a great actor to create the illusion of age, or nationality, or station in life, without once resorting to a beard, false teeth or whatever. External devices should be used merely to help an audience believe the role, not to help an actor to play it."

Seven Faces premiered at the Roxy Theatre in New York to very mild reviews. In order to help "ballyhoo" the project, Muni was sent to the theater to make a stage appearance after each showing. He appeared only once. The insecure actor had never been "himself" in front of such a large audience before and was so nervous that he could hardly speak.

The picture was a disaster in almost every respect. Muni, unhappy at the way the film had been cut, returned to Hollywood completely disenchanted with the movies. Conversely, the powers at Fox had a similar attitude toward him.

Albert Lewis visited the Munis one Sunday to find them packing. Said the actor to his friend: "They'll have to sue me if they want to pick up my option!" With that, the couple loaded their belongings into their car and drove back to New York.

Winfield Sheehan's reaction to the departure was, "Good riddance!"

The actor was still in demand on Broadway and, in October of 1930, opened at the Morosco Theatre as Saul Holland in Sidney R.

Publicity shot from *Seven Faces.*

Buchman's *This One Man.* It was staged by Leo Bulgakov and produced by Arthur Lubin and Richard W. Krakeur.

Muni played a safecracker who allows his brother to be executed for a murder he committed. The play received mixed notices and closed at the end of five weeks.

However, Muni's performance was highly praised. According to Brooks Atkinson in the *New York Times:* "As Saul, the unregenerate, Mr. Muni is overpowering and magnificent. He is an actor of virtuosity, with a variety of vocal inflection and great physical stamina. In his acting, Saul becomes a character of many qualities—fright, rage, bravado, perplexity and remorse. Mr. Muni discriminates. He can play like a caged lion when he has to, but he can also retreat from destiny like a man stunned with fear. He has a considerable career behind him. That is all the more reason for believing that he has a great career ahead."

In February of 1931, Muni opened in Kenneth Raisbeck's *Rock Me, Julie* at the Royale Theatre, under the staging of James Light. Morris Green and Lewis E. Gensler produced the play, which ran for only seven performances.

Muni was Steven Moorhead, the illegitimate son in a Midwestern family. Atkinson of the *New York Times* said of the actor: "Paul Muni's solid personality and the candor of his acting bring something of reality to the part of the adopted boy."

Scarface was a property that had been kicking around Hollywood for some time with no studio wanting to touch it. *Little Caesar* had not been released yet and producers did not think the public would buy a gangster film. Finally, agent Al Rosen, who was representing the project, convinced Howard Hughes that *he* should film the screenplay, which was patterned after the career of mobster Al Capone.

The first problem was to find somebody to play the leading character. Rosen remembered Muni's work in both *We Americans* and *The Valiant* and suggested his name to the wealthy young producer. Hughes was not familiar with the actor, but, after an all-night sales pitch from Rosen in a Hollywood restaurant, he agreed to a screen test.

Rosen flew to New York and, together with his associate, Milton Lewis (Albert Lewis's brother), went to see Muni about the film. The actor's initial response was a flat refusal. He'd been to Hollywood and the experience had left a sour taste in his mouth.

It was Bella (she was by then more or less managing her husband's career) who changed his thinking. She liked the script and realized that this film could be an important one.

The picture, filmed under the direction of Howard Hawks, was eventually released by United Artists. The cast included Ann Dvorak, Karen Morley, Osgood Perkins, George Raft, and Boris Karloff.

When the Hays Office saw the completed picture, it objected to several elements that appeared to glorify Muni's gangster characterization of Tony Camonte. Release was held up for over a year, while some scenes were cut and new sequences, including a different ending,

Counsellor-at-Law.

were filmed. Neither Hawks nor Muni would cooperate in accomplishing the changes.

The picture was finally released in April of 1932 and received excellent reviews from critics around the country, as well as huge box-office grosses. It gave a tremendous career boost to both Muni and George Raft, who went on to become one of the screen's top tough guys. Most film historians agree that *Scarface* was the *best* of the early gangster pictures.

While *Scarface* was having its censorship troubles, Muni went back to Broadway to star in what was to be his greatest stage success. Elmer Rice's *Counsellor-at-Law* opened on November 7, 1931 at the Plymouth Theatre with Muni doing the role of self-made, Jewish, New York attorney, George Simon. The play was staged and produced by the author.

Counsellor was a total success and had a long run of 378 performances on Broadway. In his review of the production, Atkinson of the

1932: Radio broadcast from the Warner lot. From left: Robert Goldstein, Helen Vinson, Joe E. Brown, Lloyd Bacon, Jack Warner, Edward G. Robinson, Mervyn LeRoy, Bebe Daniels, Ken Murray, Muni, Glenda Farrell.

New York Times said: "Mr. Muni gives one of those forceful and inventive performances that renew faith in the theatre."

With two hits under his belt, Muni was "hot." He signed an exclusive long-term contract with Warner Brothers, which paid him fifty thousand dollars per film, and gave him script approval and the right, between pictures, to act on the stage.

In the summer of 1932, the actor returned to Hollywood to make his first film under the new agreement. Otto Kruger filled in for him in *Counsellor-at-Law.*

The picture was the classic *I Am a Fugitive from a Chain Gang,* a shocking exposé of life in Southern prison camps, which was based on a true story by Robert E. Burns. As James Allen, an innocent man sentenced to a long term on a chain gang, Muni gave what some observers consider to be his finest screen performance and earned his second Academy Award nomination.

Whereas, in the screen credits, authorship of the script for *Fugitive* is attributed to Howard J. Green and Brown Holmes, most film historians agree that Sheridan Gibney was a major contributor. Reflects Gibney: "I'd had a dispute with one of the 'powers' at the studio and, to punish me, he took my name off the credits before the film's release. Unfortunately, there was no protection for writers in those days."

Mervyn LeRoy, who directed, remembers the rock-quarry sequence: "It was, what I call, the 'Raise 'em high' scene, where the prisoners were breaking up rocks with their sledge-hammers. Muni was swinging his sledge a little too leisurely to please me, so I yelled down to him, 'Muni, you're swinging that hammer like a fag!' That did it. He gave me the dirtiest look. But, in the next take, I got what I wanted."

After he finished *Fugitive,* Muni returned to New York to resume his role in *Counsellor-at-Law.* He subsequently took it on tour, then returned to Broadway for a final two-week engagement.

Following the play's close, Muni and Bella moved to Los Angeles, taking up residence in the San Fernando Valley. He was not to be seen again on the New York stage until 1939.

His second film at Warner Brothers gave Muni the opportunity as Orin Nordholm Jr. to age from a Dakota farm boy to a retired Chicago meat-packing king in his seventies. *The World Changes,* based on Sheridan Gibney's story, *America Kneels,* was also directed by LeRoy and had in its cast Aline MacMahon, Mary Astor, Donald Cook, Margaret Lindsay, and Guy Kibbee. The narrative told how the basic values of the pioneer families eroded thru four genera-

Brother Joseph Weisenfreund, Muni, and Mary Astor on the set of *The World Changes.* Weisenfreund was an extra in a party sequence.

tions, which, Gibney suggests, contributed, partially, to the 1929 stock-market crash. The picture was not a success, due, for the most part, to a slowly paced screenplay. Muni, however, received glowing reviews from the critics.

Next, LeRoy sold him on the idea of doing a comedy. According to the director, "Muni didn't turn down many scripts that I showed him, mainly because I never brought him anything I didn't think he'd do."

The film, *Hi, Nellie,* was released in 1934. Muni played Samuel Bradshaw, a newspaper editor demoted to writing a "lonelyhearts" column. Also in the cast were Glenda Farrell, Douglass Dumbrille, and Ned Sparks. It was a minor effort, but Muni had fun making it.

Publicity shot for *Hi, Nellie.*

His first of two pictures with Bette Davis (the only *important* star he ever worked with on the Warner lot) was the 1935, release, *Bordertown,* which was directed by Archie Mayo. It was a well-done social melodrama, with Muni playing an inexperienced Mexican lawyer, Johnny Ramirez, who is disbarred and, later, becomes a partner in a gambling casino on the U.S.-Mexican border.

Western writer Rex Beach approached Muni about this time in

Publicity shot from *Bordertown.*

an effort to get him to star in a film version of one of his stories, "Don Careless." The property had been the basis of a silent picture starring Rudolph Valentino, *A Sainted Devil.* Muni declined, explaining that he felt romantic roles were "out of his reach."

Instead, the actor chose to do another social drama, *Black Fury,* a coal-mining story to be directed by Michael Curtiz. The screenplay was based on a true incident and tells of the murder of a miner by coal-company police.

Muni had had correspondence in 1933 with writer Sherwood Anderson (*Winesburg, Ohio*) about the possibility of his working on the then-untitled screenplay of a film dealing with coal mining. Evidently, the deal was never consummated, since the script for *Black Fury* was written by Abem Finkel and Carl Erickson.

It was an excellent film in all respects, with Muni garnering his usual fine notices from the critics and receiving solid support from Karen Morley, William Gargan, John Qualen, and Barton MacLane.

His following picture was *Dr. Socrates,* an exciting but unimportant melodrama, which had him playing Dr. Lee Caldwell, a surgeon forced to treat a notorious group of gangsters. Ann Dvorak and Barton MacLane played the secondary roles and William Dieterle directed from an original story by W. R. Burnett. Muni always considered the film one of his poorest efforts.

On November 3, 1935, the actor, in an interview with the *Los Angeles Times,* listed a number of roles he wanted to do in films, but couldn't, because of censorship considerations. These parts included: Francis Ferriter, a religious fanatic, who murders a streetwalker in *The Puritan* by Liam O'Flaherty; the tramp in Tom Kromer's *Waiting For Nothing,* dealing with class struggle; Mose in Robert Rylee's *Deep Dark River,* which had to do with racial problems; the seminary rector in E. L. Voynick's *The Gadfly,* concerning the revelation of secrets of the confessional; *Looms of Justice* by Rudolph Lothar—mercy killing; and *Fatherland,* Karl Billinger's novel of Hitler's Germany.

After *Dr. Socrates,* Muni turned down most of the scripts submitted to him by the studio. He didn't want to do any more routine program pictures, and that was all he was being offered.

It was producer Henry Blanke who brought Muni a screenplay from the studio files, which he liked immediately. The project was *The Story of Louis Pasteur.*

The studio didn't share the enthusiasm for *Pasteur,* but, to placate their star, agreed to order script changes as he had requested. Six rewrites later, Muni, Blanke, and director William Dieterle, who had by then also gotten behind the project, presented it again to the decision-makers, only to get a flat rejection.

As a last resort, Muni threatened to sit out the balance of his contract and do nothing unless the film was produced. (Under the terms of his deal, the studio would submit the actor three scripts as possibilities for his next film and, should he reject them, he would then submit three of his own choices. If the studio did not accept any of his, Muni would go on half-salary and do nothing for the duration of his contract.) Not wanting to lose the services of such a valuable star as Muni, Warner Brothers consented and allocated a minimum budget and shooting schedule for the project.

Sheridan Gibney wrote the Oscar-winning screenplay with Pierre Collins. He remembers that "the budget for *Pasteur* was so 'tight,' we were forced to utilize several standing sets. In one instance, a

Bette Davis, Victor McLaglen, Muni (with Oscar for *Louis Pasteur*), and Jack Warner.

On location for *The Good Earth.*

redressed Busby Berkeley set became the palace of Napoleon III."

Muni was in top form as the French scientist who discovered the cures for anthrax and rabies. His supporting cast included Josephine Hutchinson, Anita Louise, Donald Woods, and Fritz Leiber.

Pasteur was the sleeper of the year. It received rave notices, did an excellent box office, and won for Muni the Academy Award for Best Actor of 1936.

Muni's Oscar tribute came as a surprise to the Hollywood film colony. Most observers had predicted that the Award would go to either Gary Cooper for *Mr. Deeds Goes to Town* or Spencer Tracy in *San Francisco.* Victor McLaglen, winner for the previous year (*The Informer*), presented the statuette. Muni began his acceptance: "I have the greatest thrill in my life in getting this." He went on to express his deep gratitude and promised to work for future Academy honors.

Irving Thalberg then offered Muni the challenging role of Wang Lung in *The Good Earth,* which was to be filmed at Metro-Goldwyn-Mayer. Warner Brothers agreed to the loan-out and the actor moved over to the Culver City studio for his first and only picture at that lot.

The original director for the film version of Pearl Buck's novel was George Hill, who prepared the production and took a second unit to China to shoot a considerable amount of background footage. However, prior to the start of principal photography, Thalberg dismissed the director because of a personal problem that was affecting Hill's ability to perform his duties properly. He was replaced by Sidney Franklin. Then, midway through the filming, Thalberg died, and his associate, Albert Lewin, took over the producing reins.

The finished picture was hailed by both the critics and the public as being a cinema masterpiece. Muni was excellent, especially in his early scenes, but it was co-star Luise Rainer who ran away with the notices. She received her second Academy Award for the project.

During the filming of *The Good Earth,* writer Pearl Buck interested Muni in the plight of the Chinese people. In 1940, the actor contributed generously to help establish the Chinese Emergency Relief Committee, formed to aid war victims in that country. Miss Buck was a founder of that organization.

Muni agreed to do his next film, *The Woman I Love,* partly as a favor to his friend, producer Albert Lewis. It was also on a loan-out, but, this time, for RKO. The picture, based on a French production, *L'Equipage,* had the actor playing a World War I pilot. Anatole Litvak directed the cast, which included Miriam Hopkins, Louis Hayward, and Colin Clive. With the exception of some flying sequences, the film had little to recommend it.

After the surprise success of *The Story of Louis Pasteur,* it was only natural that Warner Brothers would want to put Muni into another prestige biography. With the Nazi threat in Europe becoming more ominous every day, a good choice of subject seemed to be Emile Zola, the French novelist and reformer, who spent his career fighting for the cause of truth and freedom. The screenplay by Heinz Herald, Geza Herczeg, and Norman Reilly Raine seemed to tackle the important issues of Zola's day, which were just as valid in the late 1930s.

Released during the summer of 1937, *The Life of Emile Zola,* directed by Dieterle, was Muni's greatest film triumph. The studio billed him as *Mr.* Paul Muni and critics around the country called his performance the finest of his career. The New York Film Critics named him the year's Best Actor and he also received his fourth Academy Award nomination. The actor lost the Oscar that year to Spencer Tracy; however *Zola* won for Best Picture, Best Screenplay, and Best Supporting Actor (Joseph Schildkraut).

In September of the same year, Muni was named to the Jewish Hall of Fame as one of the world's 120 greatest living Jews. The poll had been conducted by Jewish students in Chicago. A few days later, the actor was appointed to the Board of the Hollywood Anti-Nazi League for the Defense of American Democracy.

The studio began suggesting other biographical subjects for the actor. At various times, he was mentioned in connection with projected films on Victor Hugo, Anatole France, Colonel Gorgas, Haym Solomon, Lincoln, Napoleon, and Sam Houston. But Muni would have no part of them, feeling that Pasteur and Zola were too similar for repetition.

On October 4, 1937, the Munis sailed for New York on the Grace liner Santa Paula, on the first leg of a vacation that would take them to parts of Europe and Palestine. As the actor told the press upon his departure, he was looking for "objective viewpoints and a refreshing perspective."

The following January, he was briefly hospitalized in a Budapest sanatorium, after suffering a slight attack of tonsillitis.

Muni and Bella returned to Hollywood in March of 1938. Due to the success of *Zola,* he was one of the hottest actors in town and was able to renegotiate his contract at Warner Brothers. The new deal (according to the press, it was "one of the most elastic contracts ever drawn" with the studio) called for Muni to appear in eight pictures over a period of four to eight years at one hundred thousand dollars per film. Of course, he retained the right to reject any script.

Again, rumors began to circulate as to what the actor's next project would be. The most frequently mentioned titles were: *The Sea Wolf* (later filmed with Edward G. Robinson), *O. O. McIntyre, Life of Victor Hugo, Panama Canal,* and *St. Michele.* Unfortunately, Muni's ultimate choice for his picture to follow *Zola* was not a good one.

When it was first announced, *Juarez* sounded like it would be an exciting production. It was another Muni biography to be directed by Dieterle . . . this time with a very high budget. It was based, in part, on a play by Franz Werfel, and the supporting cast, including Bette Davis, Brian Aherne, Claude Rains, Gale Sondergaard, John Garfield, Donald Crisp, and Gilbert Roland, was most impressive.

Nevertheless, the elements did not "mix." The basic problem was an uneven screenplay, which moved back and forth between two antagonists who never confronted each other. Muni was good as the Mexican president, Benito Juarez, as were Brian Aherne and Bette Davis as Maximilian and Carlota. On the other hand, John Garfield was completely out of place as General Diaz. The picture did poorly at the box office.

Muni's final picture for Warner Brothers, *We Are Not Alone,* was an excellent production, based on a novel by James Hilton. The actor played a doctor in a small British village, who is accused of murdering his wife. Jane Bryan and Flora Robson co-starred in the film, directed by Edmund Goulding.

Although the picture was highly praised by critics around the country, the public stayed away, making the project a complete financial flop. Producer Henry Blanke suggests that the film's failure was due to the fact that its subject matter paralleled too closely the deteriorating European situation in 1939 and that audiences found this too depressing. Also, the story had a very downbeat ending, with the hero and heroine being hanged for a crime they did not commit.

Prior to the release of *We Are Not Alone,* Muni signed to do his first play on Broadway since *Counsellor-at-Law.* The show was Maxwell Anderson's *Key Largo,* and it bore only a slight resemblance to the Humphrey Bogart/Edward G. Robinson film of the same name, which was produced in 1948.

The show opened at the Ethel Barrymore Theatre on November 27, 1939, under the direction of Guthrie McClintic. The cast included Jose Ferrer, Karl Malden, James Gregory, Uta Hagen, and, later, as a replacement, Tom Ewell.

The play received mixed reactions from the critics. Nevertheless, Muni, as King McCloud, the guilt-ridden soldier who confronts a ring of mobsters in a hotel on a Florida key, got his usual good notices. Said Richard Lockridge in the *New York Sun:* "Mr. Muni acts the role of McCloud magnificently. He holds the character, and through the character the play, firmly in his hands. There is immeasurable sureness in his playing, and a depth of understanding of Mr. Anderson's Hamlet-like character."

Key Largo had a relatively short run in New York. However, to help recover the financial investment, Muni and most of the original cast went on the road for several weeks, taking over three railroad cars to transport them from city to city. Karl Malden recalls an incident that took place while the train was about to depart Washington D.C. for Denver: "There was an actor in the cast that had a drinking problem and, who didn't like Muni. On the night we were leaving Washington, he was about fifteen minutes late for the train. Muni told the conductor to wait a few minutes longer.

"About a block up the train platform, we saw two porters running along, pushing two baggage carts. One contained this actor's suitcases and, on the other, rode the actor . . . stinking drunk . . . shouting the most vile insults at Muni. Seeing him coming, Muni jumped on

Key Largo.

the train and yelled to the conductor, 'Start now!' "

Muni's performance in the play won him the Drama League Award for the outstanding performance of the season (1939-40). In addition, just prior to the play's opening on Broadway, the Actors' Fund of America presented him with a Certificate of Life Membership.

Before he had gone to New York, Muni had been planning with Warner Brothers to do a film biography on the life of Beethoven. But, when he arrived in Los Angeles with the *Key Largo* company to perform at the Biltmore Theatre, the studio executives informed him that *We Are Not Alone* was a box-office failure and suggested that he consider *High Sierra* as an alternative to the biography. The consensus at Warners was that the crime melodrama by W. R. Burnett would be a better financial risk.

Muni thought that *High Sierra* was a good script, but he didn't want to do another gangster role. In a phone conversation with Jack Warner, the studio head gave the actor a "take it or leave it" ultimatum and Muni got angry. He called Warner a "bastard!"

"*Mr.* bastard to you," was Warner's retort.

That evening, Muni went home and ripped up his contract with the studio. According to Bella: "He did somersaults in the living room. He jumped up and down, yelling, 'No one owns me! I'm a free man!' "

Muni felt that Warner Brothers had broken their word to him, in that they were trying to force him to do a project he had rejected.

Director Irving Pichel and Muni on location for *Hudson's Bay*.

1941: Reunion with actors of the Yiddish Theatre. From left: Aaron Lebedeff, Muni, Hymie Jacobson, Michal Michalesko, Irving Grossman, and Judah Bleich.

He demanded a release from his contract and the studio, concluding that the actor had become more trouble than he was worth, agreed to a settlement. On July 19, 1940, Muni was a free agent.

After *Key Largo* closed, Muni made a one-picture deal with 20th Century Fox to star as Pierre Radisson, the French fur trader and explorer, in *Hudson's Bay*. It was his first outdoor/adventure story and he felt it would be a good change of pace. On the other hand, it was an opportunity to prove to Jack Warner that he could always find work. (He had played this same "game" with Maurice Schwartz in the Yiddish Art Theatre. Whenever the two argued, Muni would quit and immediately go to work for a lesser Yiddish company until Schwartz asked him to come back. It was the actor's way of "thumbing his nose" at the producer.)

The film was directed by Irving Pichel and had Gene Tierney, Laird Cregar, John Sutton, and Vincent Price in supporting roles. It suffered from a weak screenplay that emphasized talk instead of action. Muni, although entertaining to watch, played his role a bit too broadly and wasn't at his best. The project was poorly received by both critics and the public.

On December 30, 1940, the actor broke his ankle at Yosemite, while skiing at Badger Pass. The injury kept him virtually inactive during the first part of the following year.

However, during his convalescence, there were offers, which he did not accept:

In June of 1941, Mrs. Gerd Grieg approached Muni regarding his playing Norwegian composer Edvard Grieg in a screen biography.

The following month, director Herman Shumlin asked the actor to star in the road company of Lillian Hellman's hit play, *Watch on the Rhine*. Muni declined, stating that he felt Paul Lukas's performance could not be equalled.

His next professional appearance was not until April 15, 1942, when he opened on Broadway for the Theatre Guild in Emlyn Williams's short-lived *Yesterday's Magic*. It was staged by Reginald Denham and had Jessica Tandy and Alfred Drake in the cast.

Muni was Maddoc Thomas, a broken-down actor, who is given a chance to reestablish himself by playing *King Lear*. Coincidentally, Muni had refused an opportunity from the Theatre Guild to star in that Shakespearean tragedy a year before.

Both the play and Muni received poor notices. Said Atkinson of the *New York Times:* "He [Muni] is giving an elaborately detailed performance. But to this playgoer, it is uninspired, better suited for an academic thesis than for an evening's pleasure in the theatre. By taking the part literally, Mr. Muni catches Mr. Williams on his weakest side."

Next, Muni signed with Columbia Pictures to star in an exciting war film dealing with the Norwegian resistance against the Nazi occupation. John Farrow directed *The Commandos Strike at Dawn,* which had Anna Lee, Lillian Gish, Cedric Hardwicke, and Alexander Knox in support.

It was a good action picture, with Muni contributing an "o.k." performance in an undemanding role.

He returned to Broadway on November 24, 1942 for a revival of *Counsellor-at-Law* at the Royale Theatre. Once again, the play was directed by author Elmer Rice. Both critics and the public were receptive to the production, which ran until the following July. Lewis Nichols in the *New York Times* said: "The evening, of course, is Mr. Muni's. With a soft voice and a loud roar, with quietness, gentleness and fierceness in turn he dominates the role as though he had started with it years before, as a child selling papers on the East Side, and had risen with it to the Fifth Avenue office of Simon and Tedesco. In the one role he is seven or eight Paul Munis, smooth and accurately setting forth as many phases as there are types crossing the threshold of the office. He is the 'Counsellor-at-Law,' no exception being granted."

On February 10, 1943, Muni was hospitalized briefly for treatment of neuritis.

Commandos Strike at Dawn.

1942: With brother Joseph Weisenfreund at his niece's wedding.

The following month, at Madison Square Garden, he acted as principal narrator of *We Will Never Die,* the dramatic mass memorial for the two million Jews killed in Europe.

Frank Borzage was in New York filming his *Stage-Door Canteen* during this period and Muni agreed to play himself in a short scene. This "musical" tribute to the service canteens boasted an all-star cast, since eighty percent of the profits from the picture were to go to help support the canteens operated by the American Theatre Wing.

Like many stars of his stature, Muni helped at home in the war effort by making hospital tours and doing Armed Forces Radio programs.

Columbia Pictures then offered Muni the role of Professor Joseph Elsner, the teacher of composer Frederic Chopin, in what was eventually titled, *A Song to Remember*. Studio head Harry Cohn did not have too much faith in the project's potential and was hesitant to pay the actor's usual high price for his services. Muni wanted to do another biography, so he agreed to take a percentage of the picture in lieu

1944: With Martha Scott and Capt. Joseph T. McKeon, as they discuss an upcoming broadcast over the Blue network for Armed Forces Radio.

1944: With Bella at the premiere of Paramount's *The Story of Dr. Wassell.* Proceeds from the event were donated to Naval Aid Auxiliary.

With Marguerite Chapman on the set of *Counter-Attack.*

of a portion of his fee. It was a wise decision, because the production was a huge success.

The project was Muni's first and only color picture. Charles Vidor directed a cast that included Merle Oberon, Cornel Wilde, and Nina Foch.

Muni was unhappy while making the picture and his performance suffered. Most critics agreed he played without restraint and that director Vidor should have taken a firmer hand with him.

He did another war film for Columbia, *Counter-Attack,* released in 1945. Muni and Marguerite Chapman played Russian soldiers, trapped in a bombed-out cellar with seven Germans. Zoltan Korda was the director and the supporting cast included Larry Parks, Philip Van Zandt, George Macready, and Rudolph Anders.

It was a very good drama, with the actor turning in a first-rate performance. Unfortunately, the film's box office was nothing to get excited about.

Bella Muni had been banned by Harry Cohn from the set of *A Song to Remember,* which was part of the reason for her husband's weak performance in that film. But, she was back again for *Counter-Attack.* She stood behind the camera for the entire shooting schedule. If she didn't like something Muni was doing, she let him know and he asked for a retake. Zoltan Korda may not have liked having another "director" on the set, but he put up with it.

Muni began to realize about this time that, although he was still probably the most highly respected artist in films, he was no longer considered a good financial risk to producers. With the exception of *A Song to Remember,* which had a lot more going for it than just his presence, none of his last few films had come even close to the grosses of *The Life of Emile Zola.* Aside from the practical considerations that would affect his career, Muni and Bella knew that he needed a commercially successful film to help strengthen his depressed ego.

He chose to play another gangster, this time in a comedy/fantasy by Harry Segall, author of the classic *Here Comes Mr. Jordan. Angel on My Shoulder* was directed by Archie Mayo for United Artists and co-starred Anne Baxter and Claude Rains.

Whereas the finished picture was quite entertaining in its own right and boasted a good Muni performance, it suffered from comparison to Segall's earlier success and did not make a good showing at the box office.

On September 6, 1946, Muni returned to Broadway to star at the Alvin Theatre in *A Flag Is Born,* presented by the American League for a Free Palestine. The play was written by Ben Hecht, with music by Kurt Weill. Luther Adler staged the production, which had Celia Adler, Marlon Brando, Jonathan Harris, and Steve Hill in the cast. Quentin Reynolds acted as narrator.

Muni played an old Jew, who sets out with his wife for Palestine. The actor worked free of charge in the play, as did the rest of the cast, with proceeds (one million dollars) going to the State of Israel. The production ran for three months in New York, then went on tour, with Jacob Ben-Ami replacing Muni.

Of Muni's performance, Brooks Atkinson of the *New York Times* said: ". . . Mr. Muni is giving one of the great performances of his career. He is always a supreme technician; he has long since mastered the language of the stage. But, he is also a man of mind and understanding. Without sentimentality, without heroics he is speaking for the Jewish race with an actor's eloquence."

Muni's only professional activity in 1947 was a summer stock production of *Counsellor-at-Law* at the Marble Head Playhouse in Marble Head, Massachusetts. Marc Daniels directed. It was a successful engagement and he returned later in the same season to repeat the role for a few extra weeks.

The following year, he again reprised the role of George Simon

With Anne Baxter at the cast party for *Angel on My Shoulder.*

1946: Testifying before a Los Angeles Coroner's Jury that investigated the death of Edward Gray, a studio grip who fell from a catwalk at the *Angel on My Shoulder* cast party.

A Flag Is Born.

in *Counsellor-at-Law.* However, this time it was on television. The live video adaptation, budgeted at $17,000, was presented by *Philco Playhouse* over NBC. The experience was an unhappy one for the actor, because the requirements of the new medium did not allow him as much rehearsal time as he would have liked.

In March of 1948, Muni announced that he had optioned *Sunday Breakfast,* an original play by Emery Rubio and Miriam Balf. He planned to both produce and star in the show the following season, but his project was never realized. ANTA later produced the play in New York during May of 1952.

About the same time, producer Edward Gross told the press that he wanted the actor to star for him in *The Man Who Swindled Goering,* based on the life of Hans von Meegeren. This production never came off either.

A month later, Muni and Bella went to Goeteborg, Sweden, to research the life of Alfred Nobel, the inventor of dynamite and founder of the Nobel Prize. This was another potential film that never got before the cameras.

On February 4, 1949, Muni announced to the New York press that he was quitting films because "what they're making out in Hollywood now is just plain nonsense.

"People tell me that fine pictures are being made. When I ask them how many fine pictures are being made, they say 5 or 6 a year—5 or 6 a year out of 300! Listen, if a man set out deliberately to make poor pictures, to have something bad in every one—even with such a plan he couldn't help making 5 or 6 good ones out of 300 by mistake."

In the same interview, he went on to say: "I have never liked acting. And I never got any fun out of the excitement of Hollywood . . . little children bringing me pieces of paper and asking me to sign my name—that doesn't impress me."

The actor opened on Broadway at the Music Box Theatre on February 16 in a revival of Sidney Howard's *They Knew What They Wanted,* produced by John Golden and directed by Robert Perry. The cast included Carol Stone, Edward Andrews, Charles Kennedy, and Henry Burk Jones.

Critics were not enthusiastic about the play, which they thought had dated considerably since its 1924 production with Richard Bennett and Pauline Lord. Nor were they happy with Muni's performance as Tony, the middle-aged Italian wine grower. As John Chapman said in the *Daily News,* "Mr. Muni makes the most of it [the play], with a characterization of an Italian peasant, which is so perfect in its detail that it looks unreal. Most Italians can't act as Italian as Mr. Muni acts."

On April 15, 1949, CBS Radio, in cooperation with the United Jewish Appeal, presented *This Year Israel,* a special Passover drama. Muni was the star of the program, which was broadcast from New York.

They Knew What They Wanted closed after two months and, shortly thereafter, Muni signed to star in the London company of Arthur Miller's hit play, *Death of a Salesman.* The drama opened on August 7, 1949, to generally good reviews. W. A. Darlington, London correspondent to the *New York Times,* reported: "Paul Muni plays Willy [Loman] with great feeling. On the opening night, he seemed to be endowing the little man with a hesitating manner, which, for a time, passed muster as a piece of characterization, but in the end came under suspicion of being the artist's cloak for an imperfect acquaintance with his words. Either way, Muni's acting will be better when he has tightened up a little."

The play ran in London until January 28 of the following year, when Muni quit because he was "too tired to go on with it."

He was professionally inactive for about two years. Most of this period was spent in seclusion at his San Fernando Valley home, reading and, in general, taking life easy.

In 1952, he journeyed to Italy to film *Stranger on the Prowl* for director Joseph Losey. He did not enjoy working in that country and the completed picture was a disappointment to everyone involved. It received a limited release in the United States through United Artists.

When he returned to California, George Raft visited Muni at his home on several occasions to discuss the possibility of the pair doing a sequel to their previous success, *Scarface.* Muni liked the idea at first, recalls Raft, "but then seemed to lose interest in it. I guess he was having too much fun making plastic ashtrays."

In the spring of 1953, Muni had his first experience working in *filmed* television. Producer/director/writer Arthur Dreifuss had approached the actor with regard to doing a thirty-minute episode of the Screen Gems anthology series, "Ford Theatre." The segment, *The People vs Johnson,* was taken from *Fair Trial,* a book by Richard B. Morris of Columbia University. It was to serve as a pilot for a proposed courtroom series, which, if sold, would, hopefully, have Muni as narrator.

Muni liked Dreifuss and, since he had nothing better to do, agreed to sign for the episode, however he reserved the right to back out of doing a series, should he not enjoy working in the medium.

Muni's role in the show had him playing an attorney in a murder trial. Adele Jergens was also in the cast. Dreifuss recalls the production: "The show was shot in three days. Muni had never worked this rapidly before and he had to be constantly prompted—line by line. It was a difficult situation for everyone involved."

According to Dreifuss, there were later problems: "About the time the show was to be aired, the American Legion wrote to the advertising agency that handled the series, demanding that the segment be shelved. They claimed that Muni had contributed to a Spanish Children's Relief Fund, which later turned out to be a Communist front.

"Now, Muni was as much a Commie as are John Wayne or President Nixon. He hated the Communists. Any contributions he made were given to what he thought was a charitable cause. A lot of stars gave innocently to these organizations. Edward G. Robinson was one.

"Fred Briskin, the executive producer of the series, and I wrote to the American Legion on Muni's behalf. The matter was cleared up and the show aired on schedule."

Dreifuss had a few more discussions with Muni about doing the courtroom series, as well as one on ESP, but the actor decided that television on a regular basis was not for him.

In October of 1953, he was signed by producers James Russo, Michael Ellis, and Madeleine Clive to star in the Broadway-bound play, *Home at Seven* by R. C. Sheriff. The story had been the basis of a British film, *Murder on Monday,* starring Ralph Richardson.

The production opened for tryouts at the Astor Theatre in Syracuse, New York, on November 17, 1953. Muni was David Preston, a London bank clerk, who suffers amnesia for twenty-four hours and is suspected of a murder/robbery. Betsy Palmer was also in the cast. Said *Variety:* "The play is slowpaced and overwordy, very English in conception and technique. . . . It will still have to rely upon the personal charm and warm acting of Muni to put it over."

The show folded after the Syracuse engagement, with its failure attributed to problems in the third act.

At the beginning of 1955, Muni's "stock" was probably at the lowest point of his career. He was still a highly respected artist, who, unfortunately, had not had a *real* success, either in films or on the stage, for years. The actor would accept nothing less than a leading role in a project and producers were no longer willing to gamble with his name as their only box-office insurance. On the other hand, Muni had become very discouraged by his string of flops and was reluctant to accept the very few offers that did come his way. His ego couldn't accept another failure, so it was "safer" to retire and rest on his past success.

He was in New York on a vacation when Herman Shumlin submitted him a new play by Jerome Lawrence and Robert E. Lee, entitled *Inherit the Wind.* The story was a thinly disguised version of the sensational 1925 Scopes "Monkey" trial in Dayton, Tennessee, which matched Clarence Darrow and William Jennings Bryan against each other. Basis for the case was the fact that John T. Scopes, a school teacher, had violated a state law by daring to teach the Darwinian theory of evolution to his students.

Muni was immediately enthusiastic about the script. He felt that

Publicity shot for *Inherit the Wind.*

Inherit the Wind: Ed Begley, Tony Randall, Muni, and Louis Hector.

the elements of bigotry and thought-control that were in the play paralleled Joseph McCarthy's investigations of a few years previous and this production could serve as the actor's protest against that senator's ruthless methods. He signed to do the production with Shumlin directing. The cast included Ed Begley, Tony Randall, and Bethel Leslie. Muni, of course, played Henry Drummond, the role based on Darrow.

According to cast member Robert Lieb, "Muni arrived at the first rehearsal and feigned laryngitis. He just sat there and listened. In fact, he didn't start reading his lines until the third or fourth rehearsal.

"He confided to me later that he was 'scared' at those first few rehearsals. His last couple of plays had been flops and he wanted to be around the people he was going to work with for awhile, so he could gain a little self-confidence."

Inherit the Wind opened in New York on April 21, 1955, at the National Theatre. Reviews were excellent, with critics praising both Muni and the production. Lewis Funke of the *New York Times* said of the actor: "Credit Mr. Muni with a magnificent performance. As

Henry Drummond, the infidel from Chicago, he has one of the acting plums of his career. Back in the theatre after a six-year absence, he is giving one of the superb portrayals of the season. Not a detail has been overlooked as he gets inside the character—the shuffling gait, the unpressed suit, the ruffled gray hair, the grimace in amazement, the cunning of the trial attorney, the booming, stentorian voice of the lawyer rushing in for the kill. When Mr. Muni is on the stage, 'Inherit The Wind' is gripping and absorbing."

The play had a long run in New York and Muni won both the Donaldson and Antoinette Perry awards for his performance. It was his greatest stage success since the 1931 version of *Counsellor-at-Law* and, as Bella put it, served as his "vindication." In other words, the world knew her husband was still *number one.*

During the late summer of 1955, Muni developed a painful condition and partial loss of vision in his left eye. Four New York eye specialists diagnosed the cause of his trouble as a tumor and the actor was temporarily forced to withdraw from the play. He was replaced by Melvyn Douglas, although *his* choice for a substitute had been Karl Malden.

The tumor was malignant and Muni's eye was removed. After recovering from his initial feeling of depression, which is normal in such cases, he indicated that his greatest regret was over the fact that he would no longer be able to drive. The actor took three months to recuperate before he returned to the production.

On the night of his return, Melvyn Douglas walked out in front of the curtain prior to the performance and said: "According to the rules of Actor's Equity, an announcement must be made if an actor is to be replaced. It is my great honor to announce that tonight the part of Drummond will be played by Paul Muni."

Disappointed members of the audience, who were already halfway up the aisle to demand a refund, stopped and hurried back to their seats. As Bethel Leslie reports, "the applause was tremendous."

In retrospect, playwright Robert E. Lee feels that, of all the fine actors that played Drummond (including Douglas and Spencer Tracy), Muni's interpretation was most satisfying. According to Lee, "the greatest thing Muni had to sell was a valid anger."

March 4, 1956, found Muni on television again. He starred as an elderly senator in a half-hour drama for "General Electric Theatre," which aired over CBS. *A Letter From the Queen* was based on a story by Sinclair Lewis and co-starred Christopher Plummer and Polly Bergen.

In April of 1956, the Lambs Club in New York presented the actor with their Silver Mug, an award for "noteworthy overall contributions to the theatre." Then, in 1957, he was presented with the Albert Einstein Commemorative Award by Yeshiva University.

On March 6, 1958, Muni had his most satisfying experience in television. This time, he starred in a 1½-hour live dramatic program, entitled "The Last Clear Chance," an entry on the highly acclaimed "Playhouse 90" series over CBS. The courtroom drama was directed by George Roy Hill and written by A. E. Hotchner. Also in the cast were Lee Remick, Dick York, and Luther Adler.

According to *Variety:* "It's too early to talk about next year's Emmys and the public memory being short, the performance of Paul Muni in Thursday night's *Last Clear Chance* will pass without much notice after the plaudits have died down. The old master of the courtroom (*Inherit The Wind, Counsellor-at-Law*) doesn't come around often in TV, but when he does, he leaves his mark. To say it was a memorable performance would be repeating what has been said of most of his dramatic efforts. Suffice it to say he gave "Playhouse 90" a distinction that has been elusively absent this season.

"As an old barrister coming out of retirement to defend his son against disbarment, he etched a character laced with all the emotions of a father giving his last ounce of legal strength to save the family honor. That he came off the victor was to be expected, but the heart-rending travail that almost broke his spirit was a cameo of the dramatic art. His dressing down of the d.a., who valued his own rewards above the life of a human, guilty or not, was acting in the best tradition of the theatre."

Other critics agreed with the trade paper and Muni was nominated for an Emmy in the Best Performance by an Actor category. Fred Astaire won the honor that year for his excellent special, "An Evening with Fred Astaire." However, the dancer's win provoked considerable criticism within the television industry, the objectors feeling that Astaire should not have been placed in a competitive position with actors giving dramatic performances. The Awards structure has been changed several times since the 1959 ceremony.

What the public didn't know when they watched Muni give his brilliant *live* performance on "Playhouse 90," was that he was very insecure with his dialogue and had to be constantly prompted during the program. The hearing aid he wore on the show was actually a radio receiver, from which he was fed his lines by a prompter in the control booth.

Muni's final stage appearance was in a musical adaptation of Vicki

In the "Playhouse 90" production of "The Last Clear Chance."

At the Grand.

Baum's novel, *Grand Hotel.* It was the actor's first and only experience in musical-comedy.

At the Grand, adapted by Luther Davis, with original music and lyrics by Robert Wright and George Forrest, was produced by Edwin Lester for the Los Angeles and San Francisco Civic Light Opera programs during the summer of 1958. Albert Marre directed a cast that included Joan Diener, Cesare Danova, Nellie Adams, George

Givot, David Opatoshu, John Banner, Vladimir Sokoloff, and John Van Dreelen.

Muni played Kringelein, the middle-aged clerk out for a last fling. Lionel Barrymore had done the role in the 1932 Metro-Goldwyn-Mayer picture. The musical version also reset the action from Berlin to postwar Rome.

Although the play received only mild reviews from the West Coast press, most reviewers felt that, with some changes, it could have had a successful run in New York. Of the star, *Variety* said: "Muni is tender, whimsical and altogether engaging. His singing voice is practically nonexistent, but is lightly appealing, and his dancing efforts have charm."

Writer Luther Davis, who had conceived the project after the end of World War II, recalls that the entire experience was an unhappy one for everybody involved: "We had originally set Bert Lahr for the lead, but were unable to get the show on the boards, because producers thought he was not a big enough star.

"When we finally approached Muni, both he and Bella were enthusiastic about the idea of his doing a musical. He signed to do the show just in L.A. and San Francisco, although there were discussions regarding his going on to New York with it.

"We found him to be very inflexible to work with. He was not used to the chaos in a big musical and had never worked in blackouts or with such hot lights before. If his scene ended with a blackout, he had to be led off the stage.

"He was not willing to face the fact that, whereas he was the most important character in the show, he wasn't the *only* important one. Almost on a regular basis, he would call the composers, director, and myself very early in the morning and ask us to come over to his home, so he could suggest changes. We'd sit in his living room, while he played a tape recorder, on which he had recorded his ideas. He wanted the show rewritten *to his satisfaction,* which could mean fifty reworkings of the script. We saw the production as a musical-*comedy,* but he wanted us to turn it into a tragedy.

"When we closed in San Francisco, Roger Stevens wanted to produce the show in New York, but Muni refused to go on. Frankly, after all the bickering, we had pretty much lost our enthusiasm for it, so we let the thing die."

Columbia Pictures had been after Muni for five months to star as Dr. Samuel Ableman, the elderly Jewish physician, who treated patients in the Brooklyn slums, in their screen version of the best-selling

Gerald Green novel, *The Last Angry Man.* When he finally agreed, it was to be on his terms.

He ordered rewrites be made *to his satisfaction* on the screenplay . . . by somebody other than the novelist. He felt that Green could not be as objective as another writer might, since the leading character was based on his own father.

Another clause in the contract stated that nobody could get equal billing with Muni unless they had been starred in a film costing at least five million dollars during the past three years or unless he (Muni) waived the restriction. He did, in fact, waive it for David Wayne.

The picture was directed by Daniel Mann and had a cast that included Wayne, Luther Adler, Betsy Palmer, Joby Baker, Joanna Moore, and Billy Dee Williams.

Released in 1959, *The Last Angry Man* was an interesting, but uneven film, which did very little business at the box office. However, Muni's performance was hailed by critics all over the country. It was a great personal success and he received his fifth Academy Award nomination for his effort.

As they had after his *Inherit the Wind* triumph, offers began to come in, but he told his agent, Harold Rose, "he was through." His health was starting to fail and he was tired.

The actor had been living in New York since the start of *Inherit the Wind* rehearsals. In about 1962, he moved back to California and bought a home in Montecito, located near Santa Barbara. It was his plan to try to relax and enjoy his "retirement."

There was one last professional appearance. Marc Daniels, the director at Marble Head, Massachusetts, for *Counsellor-at-Law* was producing a filmed television series at Four Star Television for NBC, entitled "Saints and Sinners." The show had Nick Adams playing a reporter on a mythical New York City daily newspaper.

Daniels knew that Muni was back on the West Coast and asked him to do a segment of the one-hour series. As a favor to his old friend, the actor agreed to do the episode, which was written by Ernest Kinoy.

Muni played a ninety-three-year-old man, who, on his diamond wedding anniversary, decides he wants to divorce his wife, played by Lili Darvas. Once again, he had problems memorizing his dialogue. In order to bring the show in on schedule, Daniels supplied the actor with cue cards, so he could read his lines while the camera was rolling.

During the last five years of his life, Muni was constantly in poor health, his main problem being a weak heart. In 1964, he was in the

1960: In New York City apartment.

hospital for pneumonia, compounded by a cardiac condition.

Bella was also having heart trouble and, if Muni wasn't sick at a particular moment, then she was ill. Their families were constantly expecting a phone call that one or the other had passed away.

By the spring of 1967, Muni was very weak and his doctor ordered a pacemaker inserted into his heart. The device enabled him to live for a few more months.

Paul Muni died at age seventy-two in his Montecito home on August 25, 1967. Bella was at his bedside. Obituaries attributed his death to heart disorder. The funeral service was held at Hollywood Memorial Park Cemetery Chapel on August 29 with only a few Hollywood personalities in attendance. Mervyn LeRoy and Ed Begley were there, as well as one or two others. Reflects LeRoy: "It was a very disappointing turnout for such a great talent as Muni. People's memories in this town are short."

The actor left an estate of 1.2 million dollars. With the exception of a ten-thousand-dollar bequest to his disabled brother, Ellis, the entire amount went to Bella, who, shortly after her husband's death, moved to Beverly Hills.

Although she was not in good health, she began to write what was to be Muni's biography, *The Men I've Lived With.* Unfortunately, when she died on October 1, 1971, at age seventy-three, only a few pages had been completed.

Bella left half of her estate to the City of Hope Cancer Research Hospital and the balance of one-half million dollars to Brandeis University for the establishment of the Paul Muni Theatre Arts and Film Scholarship and Fellowship Fund.

A few days before he died, Muni, who sensed the end was near, called his friend, playwright Robert E. Lee, and asked him to deliver his eulogy. In his tribute, Lee said: "Someone defined God as the voice within us which keeps saying . . . 'It isn't good enough!' If that's true, then Muni has lived very close to God."

5
THE FILMS

THE VALIANT
(1929)

A Fox Production. Based on a play of the same name by Robert Middlemass and Holworthy Hall. Adaptation and dialogue by Tim Barry and James Hunter Booth. Directed by William K. Howard. Cameraman, Lucian Andriot. Released: May, 1929. 66 minutes.

Cast

James Dyke: Paul Muni; *Mary Douglas:* Marguerite Churchill; *Warden:* DeWitt Jennings; *Judge:* Henry Kolker; *Mrs. Douglas:* Edith Yorke; *Chaplain:* Richard Carlyle; *Robert Ward:* John Mack Brown. *Also:* Clifford Dempsey, George Pearce, and Don Terry.

The Film

Muni's first film role cast him as James Dyke, a convicted murderer, who goes to the electric chair denying his identity, so that his mother and sister, played by Edith Yorke and Marguerite Churchill, will not have to live down the shame of his crime. It was adapted from a popular stage play of the same name, which was written by Robert Middlemass and Holworthy Hall.

The Valiant. With Marguerite Churchill.

The Valiant was a short film, running a scant sixty-six minutes. About ten days into production, William Fox returned to Hollywood following a business trip and viewed some of the rushes. He decided that Muni lacked sex appeal and ordered production halted. Winfield Sheehan, Fox's production head, argued that, with all the sets built and about a third of the picture already shot, it wouldn't be that much more expensive to complete the film, then "shelve" it if it was a "disaster." Fox agreed, but made drastic cuts in the budget. The result was a four and one-half reel motion picture.

The picture bombed at the box office. However, Muni's performance was praised by the critics and he received his first Academy Award nomination. John Mack Brown, who was soon to become a popular cowboy actor, was also in the cast.

What the Critics Said

"Despite its fine recording and acting, the impression is inescapable that this one might better never have been produced as its theme and story is essentially too drab, agonizing and grim to appeal to the average American moviegoer as entertainment.

". . . It is not sufficiently epic to be powerful tragedy and it is too fatalistic and sorrowful to be other than depressing.

The Valiant. With DeWitt Jennings and Richard Carlyle.

"Paul Muni, the former Muni Weisenfreund of the Yiddish stage, brings to his role a wealth of humanity. He registers splendidly with utter naturalness and, while he will be difficult to cast, he should find an important niche in the talkers. His voice is rich and pleasant, his personality strong and virile, and if he is not pretty, neither is Lon Chaney or Emil Jannings, and Muni has what those fellows have not, dialog unity.

"It's going to require much smart showmanship to exploit this young Yiddish-American actor, but directed and handled intelligently, he looks like one of the legits, who will survive in the talkers."

Variety

"At the Roxy this week is a talking picture called *The Valiant,* which is blessed with considerably more originality than most screen offerings. It has keen suspense, but in the end one may not be quite satisfied that enough has been told. Nevertheless, it is left to the imagination, as was done in the original offering, a play by Robert Middlemass and Holworthy Hall.

". . . Paul Muni is splendid as the determined Dyke."

New York Times

SEVEN FACES
(1929)

A Fox Production and release. Based on Richard Connell's *Friend of Napoleon* with dialogue by Dana Burnett. Production supervisor, George Middleton. Dual direction: camera, Berthold Viertel; dialogue, Lester Lonergan. Cameraman, Joseph August. Sound, Donald Flick. Released: November, 1929. 78 minutes.

Cast

Papa Chibou: Paul Muni; *Helene Berthelot:* Marguerite Churchill; *Judge Berthelot:* Lester Lonergan; *Georges Dufeyel:* Russell Gleason; *M. Pratouchy:* Gustav von Seyffertitz.

The Film

Muni considered this picture to be the worst of his career. It had the potential of being an acting tour de force, but because of script and editing problems, as well as the performer's difficulty in adjusting to the financial requirements of Hollywood production schedules, the finished result was less than satisfactory.

Seven Faces.

The actor played Papa Chibou, the old and lonely caretaker of a Paris wax museum, who considers the wax figures to be his "family." When the owners announce that the exhibit is to close and the statues auctioned off, Chibou decides to bid his life savings for Napoleon. After being out-bid, he steals the figure and carries it through the dark Paris streets. He is, subsequently, apprehended and put on trial, but all ends well. The highlight of the picture was a dream sequence,

Seven Faces. As Svengali.

Seven Faces. As Don Juan.

in which the caretaker imagines he is several of the people (Don Juan, Svengali, Franz Schubert, Napoleon, and others) represented in the museum.

As a result of their being unsympathetic to his needs in applying the detailed makeups for his various roles in the picture, Muni had constant clashes with the production staff during filming. The actor required a certain amount of time to achieve the level of perfection *he*

Seven Faces. With Marguerite Churchill and players.

Seven Faces. With Russell Gleason.

Seven Faces. With player.

desired in creating his *Seven Faces,* however, in Hollywood, time is money and, often, there isn't enough money available to seek perfection.

Muni was also upset with the studio's publicity campaign for the film, which compared him to Lon Chaney. Said the actor in an interview: "I'm an actor. I play *any* part." That is, he regarded Chaney as a master, but whereas Chaney portrayed grotesque roles, he, Muni, did characters from ordinary walks of life.

Seven Faces was a failure in almost every respect.

What the Critics Said

"Another ordinary program picture for a good actor. Its novel aspect of ably executed wax figures, six of whom Muni plays in a dream sequence, will likely keep it alive for average grosses.

". . . In *Seven Faces,* Muni plays the aged attendant of a Parisian Mme. Tussaud's, a corking performance all the way."

Variety

"In an audible picture that, despite poor dialogue and none too imaginative direction, arouses considerable curiosity through its ingeniously conceived incidents, Paul Muni, who was last seen on the screen in the talking version of *The Valiant,* gives a sympathetic and competent characterization as Papa Chibou, the watchman in a Paris waxworks show. Mr. Muni also impersonates in the course of a dream sequence six of the lay figures under his charge who are supposed to come to life and give him advice concerning love and women. These momentary flashes of Franz Schubert; Willie Smith, a costermonger; Don Juan; Diablero, a hypnotist; and Napoleon, are not nearly so interesting, however, as the interpretation of Papa Chibou."

New York Times

SCARFACE
(1932)

A United Artists Release. Produced and supervised by Howard Hughes. Directed by Howard Hawks. Assistant Director, Richard Rosson. Based on the novel by Armitage Trail. Screenplay, Ben Hecht, Seton I. Miller, John Lee Mahin, W. R. Burnett, Fred Pasley. Photography, Lee Garmes and L. W. O'Connell. Editor, Edward Curtiss. Sound, William Snyder. Released: April, 1932. 99 minutes.

Cast

Tony Camonte: Paul Muni; *Cesca Camonte:* Ann Dvorak; *Poppy:* Karen Morley; *Johnny Lovo:* Osgood Perkins; *Guido Rinaldo:* George Raft; *Ben Guarino:* C. Henry Gordon; *Angelo:* Vince Barnett; *Pietro:* Henry Armetta; *Mrs. Camonte:* Inez Palange; *Louie Costillo:* Harry J. Vejar; *Chief of Detectives:* Edwin Maxwell; *Man-*

Scarface. With Vince Barnett and Pedro Regas.

aging Editor: Tully Marshall; *Gaffney:* Boris Karloff; *Epstein:* Bert Starkey; *Garston:* Purnell Pratt. *Also:* Paul Fix, Hank Mann, Charles Sullivan, Harry Tenbrook, and Maurice Black.

The Film

Scarface (subtitled *The Shame of the Nation*) did for Muni what *Little Caesar* and *Public Enemy* did for Edward G. Robinson and James Cagney. Of the three classic gangster melodramas, it has weathered the test of time best. Even by today's standards, it remains a fast-paced, action-filled film with superior performances and direction.

Whereas the picture was the turning point in the careers of both Muni and George Raft, the latter is probably more identified with the film today than the star. It was the ex-hoofer's first important role and he gave an impressive performance, which he was never to equal. Raft not only introduced his famous coin-flipping gimmick in the film, but almost stole the show with his sensational death scene. In later years, Raft admitted that the death scene was strictly an accident: "When Muni fired the gun, I bumped the back of my head against the corner of the set. My eyes rolled upward and I was actually knocked out for a few minutes."

The story line was loosely based on the career of "Scarface" Al Capone. Muni played Tony Camonte, vicious triggerman to mobster Johnny Lovo (Osgood Perkins). Raft was Guido Rinaldo, Carmonte's henchman, who falls in love with Tony's sister, Cesca (Ann Dvorak).

After brutally murdering numerous rival gangsters in order to keep Lovo in control of the rackets, Camonte is almost slain in a gun battle with other hoods, as they race through the streets in a thrilling automobile chase. He kills his attackers, then learns that his attempted assassination was ordered by Lovo, who feared that he (Camonte) was becoming too dangerous and unpredictable. Rinaldo executes a pleading Lovo and Camonte becomes a powerful crime czar.

Camonte's Achilles' heel is his overprotective attitude toward his sister, which camouflages an almost incestuous feeling on his part. When he learns that she is living with Rinaldo (he is not aware that they are married), he goes to their apartment and kills his associate.

The police seize this opportunity to come after Camonte and a blazing gun battle ensues, in which Cesca is slain. Camonte's demise is not long to follow.

The release of the Howard Hughes/Howard Hawks film was delayed for sixteen months because of censorship problems. Objections stemmed from the fact that the picture "glorified" the gangster. After

Scarface. With Karen Morley and Osgood Perkins.

Scarface. With George Raft and Henry Armetta.

Scarface. With George Raft.

much "discussion," several new scenes and an alternate ending were shot to placate the social critics. However, Howard Hawks refused to direct these sequences, as he was quite content with *his* finished picture.

Basically, the new scenes consisted of "moral lectures" delivered by a newspaper editor (Tully Marshall) and a chief of detectives

Scarface. With Osgood Perkins.

(Edwin Maxwell). They may have satisfied the censors, but only served to slow down the pace of the picture itself.

The ending audiences saw depended upon what part of the country they were in. The original and better of the two had a cowardly Camonte being shot down in the street by the police. The alternate consisted of him being captured, tried, convicted, given a moral lecture by the judge, and, finally, hanged. Camonte was only shown in silhouette in this version because Muni was either unavailable or did not wish to shoot it.

Boris Karloff's role in the drama was patterned after real-life gangster and Capone adversary, "Bugs" Moran.

Scarface was a huge critical and financial success. In recent years,

Scarface.

it has been withheld from re-release by Howard Hughes and has never been shown on television. However, at this writing, there are persistent rumors that the producer may soon release this cinema classic again.

What the Critics Said

"Regardless of the moral issues, *Scarface* is entertainment on an important scale.

". . . Muni, with a scar from his ear to his jaw, is Scarface. He's tough enough here to make Capone his errand boy. And convincing along with it, which has as much as anything else to do with the picture's merit."

Variety

"It is a stirring picture, efficiently directed and capably acted, but as was once said of *The Covered Wagon,* that it was all very well if you liked wagons, so this is an excellent diversion for those who like to take an afternoon or an evening off to study the activities of cowardly thugs.

"In it, Paul Muni as Scarface Tony Camonte gives a compelling portrayal. This Tony has a crossed scar on his left cheek from which he derives his sobriquet. He is a vigorous murderer with a charmed life when it comes to avoiding the bullets from rivals when he is driving an automobile. He is supposed to be responsible here for a St. Valentine's Day massacre and many other killings.

". . . the picture is dominated by Mr. Muni's virile and vehement acting."

New York Times

I AM A FUGITIVE FROM A CHAIN GANG (1932)

A Warner Brothers Production and release. Directed by Mervyn LeRoy. Based on a book by Robert E. Burns, *I Am a Fugitive from a Georgia Chain Gang*. Screenplay, Howard J. Green and Brown Holmes. Art Director, Jack Okey. Photography, Sol Polito. Editor, William Holmes. Gowns, Orry-Kelly. Technical Advisors, S. H. Sullivan and Jack Miller. Released: October, 1932. 93 minutes.

Cast

James Allen: Paul Muni; *Marie Woods:* Glenda Farrell; *Helen:* Helen Vinson; *Pete:* Preston Foster; *Barney Sykes:* Allen Jenkins; *Bomber Wells:* Edward Ellis; *Nordine:* John Wray; *Reverend Robert Clinton Allen:* Hale Hamilton; *Guard:* Harry Woods; *Warden:* David Landau; *Second Warden:* Edward J. McNamara; *Ramsey:* Robert McWade; *Prison Commissioner:* Willard Robertson; *Linda:* Noel Francis; *Mrs. Allen:* Louise Carter; *The Judge:* Berton Churchill; *Allen's Secretary:* Sheila Terry; *Alice:* Sally Blane; *Red:* James Bell; *Chairman of Chamber of Commerce:* Edward LeSaint; *District Attorney:* Douglass Dumbrille; *Fuller:* Robert Warwick. *Also:* Charles Middleton, Reginald Barlow, Jack LaRue, Charles Sellon, Erville Alderson, George Pat Collins, William Pawley, Lew Kelly, Everett Brown, William LeMaire, George Cooper, Wallis Clark, Walter Long, Frederick Burton, Irving Bacon, Lee Shumway, J. Frank Glendon, Dennis O'Keefe.

The Film

Muni's first picture for Warner Brothers was based on an autobiography by Robert E. Burns, *I Am a Fugitive from a Georgia Chain Gang*. To avoid possible legal problems, the name of the state was dropped from the film's title.

Burns, who was a technical advisor on the project, had served in a Georgia prison camp, as the result of being convicted of a five-dollar grocery store robbery. He escaped in 1922, went to Chicago, became a writer and, later, editor of a magazine. When his ex-wife revealed his identity, he was returned to Georgia despite the pleas of many prominent citizens.

He escaped a second time, then went to New Jersey to become a tax expert and write his book. Georgia again demanded his return, but three New Jersey governors refused to extradite him.

I Am a Fugitive from a Chain Gang. Lew Kelly, Muni, and Preston Foster.

I Am a Fugitive from a Chain Gang. With Harry Woods.

I Am a Fugitive from a Chain Gang. Player, Muni, Harry Woods, and David Landau.

I Am a Fugitive from a Chain Gang.

In 1945, Burns returned to Georgia on the assurance of that state's governor, Ellis Arnall, that *he* would defend the fugitive. Arnall had already done away with the state's chain-gang system. The Georgia Pardon and Parole Board commuted Burns's sentence and restored his civil rights. However, he was refused a full pardon, because of his role in the holdup. Burns died in 1955.

The Mervyn LeRoy-directed film remained fairly faithful to the book. Muni played James Allen, an honest ex-army engineer, who, after World War I, finds it difficult to earn a living. One moving scene shows him trying to pawn his military medals, only to learn they're a "drug on the market."

Allen takes to the road and is innocently involved in the holdup of a hamburger stand. He is captured and, unable to prove his innocence, sentenced to serve on a brutal chain gang, where floggings are given for the slightest infraction of the rules.

He escapes and, like Burns, goes to Chicago. He becomes a construction laborer and, over a period of years, works his way up to a top executive level. However, his vicious wife (Glenda Farrell), who actually blackmailed him into marrying her, informs the authorities

I Am a Fugitive from a Chain Gang. With Helen Vinson.

I Am a Fugitive from a Chain Gang. With Glenda Farrell.

I Am a Fugitive from a Chain Gang. With players.

I Am a Fugitive from a Chain Gang. From left: Allen Jenkins, Jack LaRue, John Wray, Edward Ellis, Player, Muni, and Harry Woods.

of his identity. He is arrested, and a legal tug-of-war between the two states ensues. Finally, on the assurance of a prison official that he will be pardoned if he serves ninety days as a trustee, Allen returns voluntarily to the Southern state.

Upon his arrival, he is double-crossed and sent back to the chain gang. He serves his ninety days, but the Parole Board then decides he must serve an entire year before he may be pardoned. When he is not released at the end of the year, he escapes a second time.

Desperately fleeing the law, Allen meets his girl friend (Helen Vinson) for a brief farewell. She asks if he will write. He shakes his head. "How do you eat?" she asks.

"I steal," he replies, as he disappears into the night.

This, one of the most shocking finales ever filmed, actually came about as the result of an accident. While rehearsing the scene in an alley in downtown Los Angeles, several lights blew out at the same time and plunged the actors into darkness. Director LeRoy liked the effect and decided to have Muni deliver his last line from a completely black screen.

I Am a Fugitive from a Chain Gang. With Helen Vinson. "I steal!"

LeRoy recalls the picture: "*Fugitive* caused both myself and Jack Warner plenty of problems. The wardens of the Georgia chain gangs weren't too happy for obvious reasons and tried to stop the picture from being shown. It did one thing, however. The chain gangs were taken off the roads in Georgia. But Warner and I were told not to come there again. I don't think that warning still holds, though."

I Am a Fugitive from a Chain Gang is still a disturbing, yet thrilling, picture to watch and it remains one of the greatest documents of social injustice ever filmed. Both the picture and Muni received Academy Award nominations.

What the Critics Said

"*I Am a Fugitive from a Chain Gang* is a picture with guts. It took lots of guts to make it, too, considering the apparent minimization of certain essential ingredients. The most necessary elements for the femme trade—the romance angle and a happy ending—are almost totally lacking here. Yet despite their lack, *Fugitive* merits and will probably achieve box-office recognition. It's a good picture. No dispute as to that. It grips with its stark realism and packs lots of punch.

". . . Everything about *Fugitive* is technically 100% from the playing and direction down. Muni turns in a pip performance."

Variety

". . . It is a vehement attack on convict camps, with most of the details culled from the book on which it is based.

"The producers do not mince matters in this melodrama, and even at the close there is none of the usual bowing to popular appeal. Several sequences are worked out with genuine suspense, and, although one might be justified in presuming that some of the cruelty is exaggerated, the sight of scores of men working with shackled ankles is enough to make much of the narrative seem credible.

"Paul Muni plays the leading role, giving a convincing and earnest performance as James Allen, an ex-sergeant in the A.E.F., who is a victim of circumstances."

New York Times

THE WORLD CHANGES
(1933)

A First National Production for Warner Brothers. A First National Release. Directed by Mervyn LeRoy. Screenplay by Edward Chodorov from Sheridan Gibney's story, *America Kneels.* Camera, Tony Gaudio. Released: September, 1933. 90 minutes.

Cast

Orin Nordholm, Jr.: Paul Muni; *Anna Nordholm:* Aline MacMahon; *Virginia:* Mary Astor; *Richard Nordholm:* Donald Cook; *Natalie:* Patricia Ellis; *Selma Peterson:* Jean Muir; *Jennifer:* Margaret Lindsay; *Claflin:* Guy Kibbee; *Paul:* Theodore Newton; *Ogden Jarrett:* Alan Dinehart; *Orin Nordholm, Sr.:* Henry O'Neill; *Mrs. Peterson:* Anna Q. Nilsson; *Buffalo Bill:* Douglass Dumbrille; *Custer:* Clay Clement. *Also:* Gordon Wescott, Arthur Hohl, William Janney, Philip Faversham, Sidney Toler, George Meeker, Mickey Rooney, Jackie Searle, Marjorie Gateson, Oscar Apfel, Alan Mowbray, William Burress, and Wallis Clark.

The Film

Muni's second film for Warner Brothers gave him the opportunity to age from a youth in his early twenties to an old man of seventy-seven.

The World Changes was a chronicle of the Nordholm family, beginning in 1852 on the plains of the Dakotas, through four generations to the stock market crash of 1929. Muni was Orin Nordholm, Jr., son of Anna (Aline MacMahon) and Orin, Sr. (Henry O'Neill), who founded the pioneer settlement of Orinville.

Upon the urging of Buffalo Bill Cody (Douglass Dumbrille), Orin, Jr. decides to leave the Dakotas and drive a cattle herd from Texas . . . North to where beef is scarce. The venture is successful and Orin becomes partners with Claflin (Guy Kibbee) in a Chicago slaughterhouse. He later meets and marries Claflin's daughter, Virginia (Mary Astor).

Time passes: Claflin dies; the Nordholms are blessed with two sons; the business prospers. Orin devises the practice of ice-packed freight cars as a method of transporting slaughtered beef and this idea makes him one of the leaders in his industry.

However, Virginia, a social climber, dislikes the meat business and urges her husband to quit it. She wants their older son, Richard

The World Changes. Director Mervyn LeRoy (in canvas chair) gives Muni final instructions.

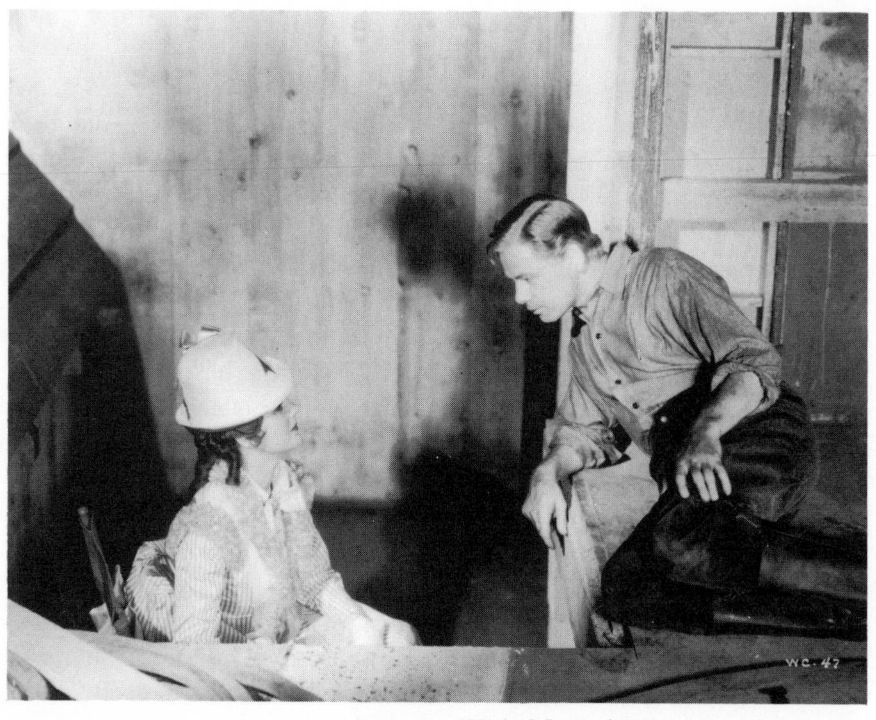

The World Changes. With Mary Astor.

The World Changes. With Jean Muir.

(Donald Cook), to marry Jennifer (Margaret Lindsay), daughter of a socially prominent New York family. At a ball held in honor of the Eastern family, Virginia announces that Orin is selling his business, an act that puts the value of the company's stock in jeopardy. Orin refuses to go along with his wife and she, subsequently, has a nervous collapse. A few days later, Virginia is a stark raving lunatic. She dies shortly thereafter. Feeling responsible, Orin sells his business and agrees to set Richard up in a stock brokerage business.

More years go by. The year is 1929. Jennifer is now Mrs. Richard Nordholm and the couple have three grown children. She is also having an affair with Ogden Jarrett (Alan Dinehart), a business associate of her husband. The stock market crashes and Richard, who has embezzled money from his firm, faces ruin, as well as prison. Orin has not approved of what his son has done with his life, but decides to utilize the remainder of his fortune to pay off Richard's investors and save the Nordholm name. Unaware of his father's actions, Richard learns of his wife's affair and kills himself. Upon discovering the body, Orin dies of a stroke.

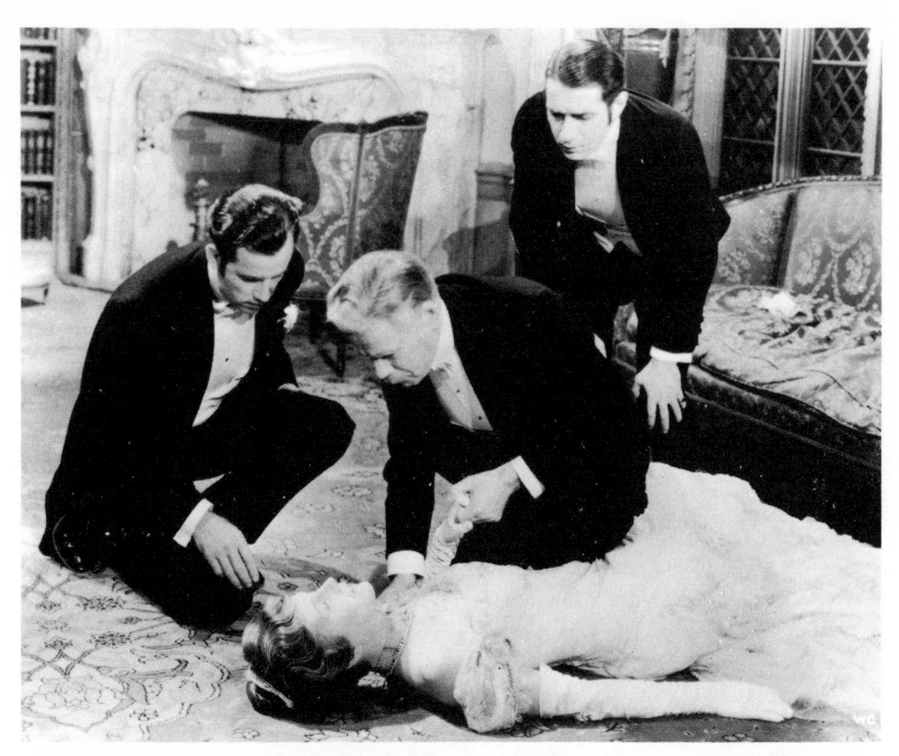

The World Changes. With Gordon Westcott, Mary Astor, and Donald Cook.

The World Changes. With Philip Faversham.

Muni had never been on a horse prior to this film and he took lessons in order to accomplish the early scenes, which were filmed near Oxnard, California.

Director Mervyn LeRoy believes that he introduced the 360-degree pan with this picture. The camera movement takes place late in the film when Anna Nordholm meets her relatives.

The World Changes.

The major problem with the production was a slow-moving screenplay, with the more interesting sequences taking place in the first half hour. However, Muni was nothing short of brilliant in each and every stage of Orin Nordholm, Jr.'s life. Although virtually ignored by film historians, it is one of his best performances. Mary Astor turned in a fine job, especially in her mad scene.

The picture's failure at the box office was due, in part, to its plot similarity to another Warner production, *I Loved a Woman,* with Edward G. Robinson and Kay Francis, which was released about the same time. It also dealt with a Chicago meat packer and his social-climbing wife.

What the Critics Said

"A fine picture, which should get money . . . it is not only a worthy prestige production that does much to bolster the credit side of the cinematic ledger, but it is completely entertaining.

"This is a cavalcade of American pioneering that majestically paints a celluloid record of the Nordholm family through 4 generations.

"Muni has turned in a masterly performance. He motivates and ages with the succession of years in realistically effective manner."

Variety

"It is a panorama of seven decades, depicting the ambition and disappointments of a family, chiefly of Orin Nordholm, who is acted by the talented Paul Muni. It goes from 1852 on the Plains of South Dakota to 1929 in the excitement of Wall Street. Its early glimpses recall *The Covered Wagon,* and many of the scenes during that period and shortly thereafter are depicted with grand effect. They possess a stirring quality. The up-to-date melodramatic episodes, however, are too lurid, too extravagant and too forced to be persuasive.

"But throughout the rolling years, there is Paul Muni as a young man, Paul Muni middle aged, and then as an old grandfather. His performance always enhances the scenes in which he appears. As an old man, his make-up and bearing are thoroughly convincing. He, as Orin Nordholm, puts real life into the story, even in some of the closing passages, for there is a genuine pathos over watching Nordholm sneering at some of the effete members of his family and hardly able to contain himself when it comes to the women with lofty social aspirations."

New York Times

HI, NELLIE
(1934)

A Warner Brothers Production and release. Directed by Mervyn LeRoy. From a story by Roy Chanslor. Adaptation by Abem Finkel and Sidney Sutherland. Photography by Sol Polito. Released: January, 1934. 75 minutes.

Cast

Bradshaw: Paul Muni; *Gerry:* Glenda Farrell; *Dawes:* Douglass Dumbrille; *Brownell:* Robert Barrat; *Shammy:* Ned Sparks; *Fullerton:* Hobart Cavanaugh; *Sue:* Pat Wing; *O'Connell:* Edward Ellis; *Sheldon:* George Meeker; *Graham:* Berton Churchill; *Louie:* Sidney Miller.

The Film

Muni's sixth picture offered him a change of pace. It was his first

Hi, Nellie.

screen comedy and, although the completed film left much to be desired, he had fun making it.

The actor was Samuel Bradshaw, the managing editor of a big city newspaper, the *Times-Star,* who is demoted following a disagreement with his publisher. Bradshaw is directed to write the paper's "lonelyhearts" column, an assignment he detests and which starts him drinking. Replacing him as editor is Harvey Dawes (Douglass Dumbrille).

A lecture from his predecessor, Gerry Krale (Glenda Farrell), makes Bradshaw pocket his pride and he goes on to make the column a huge success.

Bradshaw discovers that an influential banker has been murdered and buried under the name of another man. He breaks the story and is, subsequently, returned to his old job.

The picture received only mild reviews and did not do an impressive box office. It was not that it was a bad film . . . just not a very important one. In fact, it was similar in story content to a 1933 United Artists release starring Lee Tracy, *Advice to the Lovelorn.*

Hi, Nellie was remade by Warner Brothers in 1942. That version

Hi, Nellie. With Ned Sparks.

Hi, Nellie. With Glenda Farrell.

Hi, Nellie. With Glenda Farrell.

was called *You Can't Escape Forever* and starred George Brent and Brenda Marshall.

What the Critics Said

"Though it struggles to entertain, *Hi Nellie* fails to rise to the occasion. It is never more than casually amusing or exciting. For Paul Muni it represents another film characterization that is as clear-cut and fine as it could be. It's a better Muni performance than a picture."

Variety

". . . Mr. Muni acts his part with spontaneity and a sense of humor. The episode devoted to his drowning his sorrow with alcohol is thankfully brief, but, as Bradshaw, he hoodwinks evil-doers with remarkable ease."

New York Times

BORDERTOWN
(1935)

A Warner Brothers Production and release. Executive producer, Jack L. Warner. Directed by Archie Mayo. Screenplay by Laird Doyle and Wallace Smith. Adaptation by Robert Lord. Based on a novel by Carroll Graham. Camera, Tony Gaudio. Musical score, Bernhard Kaun. Art direction, Jack Okey. Editor, Thomas Richards. Released: January, 1935. 89 minutes.

Cast

Johnny Ramirez: Paul Muni; *Marie Roark:* Bette Davis; *Dale Elwell:* Margaret Lindsay; *Padre:* Robert Barrat; *Charlie Roark:* Eugene Pallette; *Mr. Elwell:* Henry O'Neill. *Also:* Gavin Gordon, Arthur Stone, Soledad Jiminez, William B. Davidson, Hobart Cavanaugh, Vivian Tobin, Nella Walker, Oscar Apfel, Samuel S. Hinds, Chris Pin Martin, Frank Puglia, Jack Norton, and Arthur Treacher.

The Film

With *Bordertown,* Muni returned to character roles. This time, he played an inexperienced Mexican/American lawyer, Johnny Ramirez, who is disbarred after losing his temper in the courtroom.

Ramirez takes a job as a bouncer in a bordertown casino run by Charlie Roark (Eugene Pallette). He is a definite asset to the business and the owner makes him a full partner.

Roark's wife, Marie (Bette Davis), takes a romantic interest in Ramirez, but he spurns her advances in favor of Dale Elwell (Margaret Lindsay), a society girl who enjoys slumming in the bordertown cafés and casinos.

Desperately wanting Ramirez for herself, Marie murders her husband by locking him in the garage after he has fallen asleep in a drunken stupor and leaving the car motor running. Roark's death by carbon monoxide poisoning is ruled accidental by a coroner's jury.

When Ramirez still ignores her, Marie confesses her crime to him, then goes to the police with a story, which implicates him in the murder also. They are both arrested. However, Marie proves to be unreliable on the witness stand. Her feelings of guilt about the crime have driven her to a mental breakdown and it becomes obvious to the court that she had lied about Ramirez's involvement.

Ramirez returns to the casino. In a confrontation with Dale, she mocks him for being in love with her. He tries to force his attentions on her, but she flees, only to be killed when she runs in front of an automobile. Remorseful, Ramirez sells the casino and donates the money to a school for underprivileged Mexican children.

In order to prepare for his role in the film, Muni hired a Mexican chauffeur named Manuel and spent weeks studying his gestures and

Bordertown. With Bette Davis.

Bordertown. With Robert Barrat.

Bordertown. With players.

Bordertown. With players.

Bordertown. With Bette Davis.

speech patterns. As his cousin, Sid Ellis, remembers: "Muni became Manuel."

Bordertown was the first of two films Muni was to do with Bette Davis (*Juarez* was the other) and the first of two with director Archie Mayo (*Angel on My Shoulder* came in 1946).

The socially oriented melodrama was Muni's best film since *I Am a Fugitive from a Chain Gang,* and some critics thought his best performance to date. Bette Davis was also highly praised for her courtroom scene. Box office was good.

The 1941 Warner Brothers trucking saga, *They Drive By Night,* was a partial, if uncredited, remake of the picture with George Raft, Ida Lupino and Alan Hale doing the Muni, Davis and Pallette roles.

What the Critics Said

"Paul Muni in his best screen performance and Bette Davis equalling, if not bettering, her characterization in *Of Human Bondage* . . . an interesting yarn, fine direction and boxoffice.

"Muni is a Mexican this time and does it as realistically and as effectively as he has done Italian and other characterizations in the past."

Variety

"Among the decided advantages of *Bordertown* is the circumstance that it brings Paul Muni back to the Broadway screen after a discouraging absence, permitting him to scrape the nerves in the kind of taut and snarling role at which he is so consummately satisfying. This somber chronicle of a raffish and embittered Mexican immerses itself racily in the crude, violent and gaudy life of the bordertowns. Although its skeletal plot is not unusually novel, the Warner Brothers have produced it in the lively style of screen realism, which distinguishes their melodramas. Finally, Mr. Muni brings to the photoplay his great talent for conviction and theatrical honesty, making it seem an impressive account of angry gutter ambitions."

New York Times

BLACK FURY
(1935)

A First National Production and Warner Brothers Release. Directed by Michael Curtiz. From a story by Judge M. A. Musmanno and a play by Henry R. Irving. Screenplay by Abem Finkel and Carl Erickson. Dialogue Director, Frank McDonald. Photography, Byron Haskins. Released: April, 1935. 92 minutes.

Cast

Joe Radek: Paul Muni; *Anna Novak:* Karen Morley; *Slim:* William Gargan; *McGee:* Barton MacLane; *Mike:* John Qualen; *Steve Croner:* J. Carroll Naish; *Kubanda:* Vince Barnett; *J. W. Hendricks:* Henry O'Neill; *Tommy Poole:* Tully Marshall; *Mary Novak:* Mae Marsh; *Sophie Shemanski:* Sarah Haden; *Johnny Farrell:* Joe Crehan; *Lefty:* George Pat Collins. *Also:* Willard Robertson, Effie Ellsler, Wade Boteler, Egon Brecher, Ward Bond, and Akim Tamiroff.

Black Fury. With Karen Morley.

The Film

Black Fury was another controversial drama dealing with social injustice and, like *I Am a Fugitive from a Chain Gang,* had its basis in fact.

As Joe Radek, Muni was a robust, illiterate coal miner, whose sweetheart, Anna Novak (Karen Morley), runs away with a company cop (William Gargan). Stunned, Joe goes out and starts drinking.

A detective agency that specializes in strike-breaking has placed agents in the mines to stir up discontent among the men and try to undermine the influence of the national union. At a meeting of the miners, Joe, who is very popular with his fellow workers, comes in drunk and looking for trouble. Without realizing what he is doing, he picks up the shouts of Croner (J. Carroll Naish), an agitator, and the result is that half the men withdraw from the union. Joe is elected president of a new "union" formed by the men that walk out.

The next day, these men are locked out of the mine and a fight ensues. Following this, the mine owners declare a general lockout, evict the families from company houses, and decide to break the union.

The detective agency imports dozens of strike-breakers and thugs, employed as guards, and led by McGee (Barton MacLane). Joe is blamed by the miners for their trouble and shunned.

One of the thugs attacks the daughter of a miner and she is rescued by Mike Shemanski (John Qualen). A fight follows: Joe is knocked out and Mike is killed by McGee.

While recovering in the hospital, Joe learns that the men have decided to return to work as individuals at a lower wage. Feeling responsible, he steals some dynamite and provisions and, aided by Anna, who has realized her mistake and returned, barricades himself in the mine.

He blows up the powder plant and conducts a one-man strike against the mine police force by threatening to blow up the mine unless the owners recognize the union and its demands. McGee goes into the mine after him, but is captured by Joe instead.

Days pass. The newspapers take up the case and, finally, the government steps in and the strike is settled.

Anna goes down into the mine and explains the situation to Joe, who then comes to the surface. McGee is arrested for Mike's murder. Joe is a hero and is reunited with Anna.

The film combined elements from *Bohunk,* a play by Henry R. Irving, and "Jan Volkanik," a story by Judge M. A. Musmanno, who

Black Fury.

Black Fury. With Ward Bond and player.

had been instrumental in bringing three coal-company policemen to justice for the real-life murder in 1929 of a miner in Imperial, Pennsylvania.

To prepare for his role, Muni spent a considerable amount of time in an East-coast coal town, where he acquired his dialect, as well as a fund of technical knowledge.

Vince Barnett recalls that Muni tried to keep him off the picture: "There was nothing personal in his actions, since we had been friends since *Scarface*. He just felt that, in such a serious film as *Black Fury*, there shouldn't be any comic relief. Lucky for me, Mike Curtiz disagreed with him and I stayed. There were no hard feelings on Muni's part and I worked with him again on *The Woman I Love*."

The production was highly acclaimed, when it was first released, as a bold social drama. Performances were uniformly excellent, with Muni, as usual, creating a characterization unlike he had ever done before. Although the subject matter is somewhat dated today, the picture still carries a certain "punch," which makes it well worth viewing.

Black Fury.

Black Fury. With John Qualen, Vince Barnett, J. Carroll Naish (in background), and players.

What the Critics Said

"This is the best Muni picture in many moons. Muni is at his best as a young coal miner."

Film Daily

"Muni is the fulcrum of the film."

Variety

"Hollywood, with all its taboos and commercial inhibitions, makes a trenchant contribution to the sociological drama in *Black Fury,* which arrived at the Strand Theatre yesterday. Magnificently performed by Paul Muni, it comes up taut against the censorial safety belts and tells a stirring tale of industrial war in the coal fields. Some of us cannot help regretting the film's insistent use of the white-wash brush, which enables its sponsors to be in several editorial places at the same time. But when we realize that *Black Fury* was regarded by the State Censor Board as an inflammatory social document and that it has been banned in several sectors, we ought to understand that Warner Brothers exhibited almost a reckless air of courage in producing the picture at all.

"Mr. Muni is altogether superb in all the varied scenes which describe Joe Radek's climb out of peasant obscurity to the forefront of a crisis, which he never understands.

"By all odds, *Black Fury* is the most notable American experiment in social drama since *Our Daily Bread*."

New York Times

DR. SOCRATES
(1935)

A Warner Brothers Production and release. Directed by William Dieterle. Story, W. R. Burnett. Adaptation, Mary C. McCall, Jr. Screenplay, Robert Lord. Dialogue Director, Stanley Logan. Editor, Ralph Dawson. Camera, Tony Gaudio. Released: October, 1935. 74 minutes.

Cast

Dr. Caldwell: Paul Muni; *Josephine Gray:* Ann Dvorak; *Red Bastian:* Barton MacLane; *Benn Suggs:* Raymond Brown; *Bill Payne:* Ralph Remley; *Mel Towne:* Hal K. Dawson; *Caroline Suggs:* Grace Stafford; *Muggsy:* Mayo Methot; *Greer:* Henry O'Neill; *Dr. Ginder:* Robert Barrat; *Lefty:* Marc Lawrence. *Also:* John Kelly, Sam Wren, Ivan Miller, Samuel Hinds, Helen Lowell, and John Eldredge.

Dr. Socrates. With Ann Dvorak.

The Film

Dr. Socrates marked another change of pace for Muni, whose last two films had been heavy social dramas. Based on a *Liberty Magazine* serial by W. R. Burnett of *Little Caesar* fame, the picture came at the end of Warner Brothers' cycle of gangster dramas.

Dr. Socrates. With Ann Dvorak.

Dr. Socrates. Muni, Joseph Downing, Barton MacLane, Marc Lawrence, and Olin Howlin.

Muni was Dr. Lee Caldwell, a surgeon, who has moved to a small town in an effort to forget the death of his fiancée, for which he feels partly responsible.

After he is forced to patch up a bank robber at gunpoint, the notorious Red Bastian (Barton MacLane) and his gang select Caldwell as their official doctor. He also takes an interest in Josephine Gray (Ann Dvorak), an attractive hitchhiker, considered by the townsfolk to be a gangster's moll.

Caldwell rescues Miss Gray from the mobsters by convincing them they have been exposed to scarlet fever. Instead of the serum he has promised, the doctor injects the bandits with a narcotic, which puts them to sleep, as they are preparing to resist a siege at their country-lodge hideout.

Although the picture was an entertaining and well-done melodrama, most observers agreed that it was rather insignificant compared to Muni's previous work. The actor shared this view and, in later years, always dismissed it as one of his weakest efforts.

However, the project gave him the opportunity to work for the first time with William Dieterle, who was to direct him in three of his most important films, *The Story of Louis Pasteur, The Life of Emile Zola,* and *Juarez.*

Dr. Socrates was remade by Warner Brothers in 1939 under the title of *King of the Underworld.* Kay Francis played a female surgeon in that version and Humphrey Bogart was the chief gangster.

What the Critics Said

"Arriving at the tail-end of the G-Man and gangster cycle, *Dr. Socrates* is a graceful valedictory for what has been a most interesting and successful series of pictures. It hasn't the vigor of some of its predecessors, but the constant and basic threat of violence is always present and the muscle men, who motivate the story, manage to keep it always exciting.

"For Muni, who is usually handed the tough ones, *Socrates* is an easy role, calling for little or no emotional work. For an actor of his calibre, the soft-spoken doc seems a minor effort."

Variety

Dr. Socrates. With Ann Dvorak.

"Interrupting his preoccupation with big things of the cinema, Paul Muni undertakes a bit of minor league melodrama in his new photoplay at the Strand Theatre.

"Moving through the narrative with professional competence, Mr. Muni shows himself to be an able critic of the drama by resisting any temptation to give the work a false importance in his performance."

New York Times

THE STORY OF LOUIS PASTEUR (1936)

A Warner Brothers Production. Directed by William Dieterle. Produced by Henry Blanke. Story, Sheridan Gibney and Pierre Collins. Screenplay, Sheridan Gibney and Pierre Collins. Photography, Tony Gaudio. Editor, Ralph Dawson. Released: February, 1936. 85 minutes.

Cast

Pasteur: Paul Muni; *Madame Pasteur:* Josephine Hutchinson; *Annette Pasteur:* Anita Louise; *Jean Martel:* Donald Woods; *Dr. Charbonnet:* Fritz Leiber; *Roux:* Henry O'Neill; *Dr. Rosignol:* Porter Hall; *Dr. Radisse:* Ray Brown; *Dr. Zaranoff:* Akim Tamiroff; *Napoleon III:* Walter Kingsford; *Empress Eugenie:* Iphigenie Castiglioni; *Boncourt:* Herbert Heywood; *Dr. Pheiffer:* Frank Reicher; *Dr. Lister:* Halliwell Hobbes; *Phillip Meister:* Dickie Moore; *Mrs. Meister:* Ruth Robinson; *President Thiers:* Herbert Corthell. *Also:* Frank Mayo, William Burress, Robert Strange, Mabel Colcord, Niles Welch, Leonard Mudie, Brenda Fowler, Eric Mayne, Alphonze Ethier, Edward Van Sloan, and Otto Hoffman.

The Film

Warner Brothers did not want to make *The Story of Louis Pasteur.* The screenplay, which went through six rewrites, originally came out of the studio files. Executive producer Hal Wallis was against it: "The public won't accept Muni with a beard. He'll look like a rabbi."

Jack Warner was against it: "Who wants to see a movie about bugs?"

It took the combined efforts of the actor, producer Henry Blanke, and director William Dieterle to push the project through. At that, however, the production was given a minimum budget and shooting schedule.

Muni won an Oscar for his portrayal of the French scientist, who discovered the cures for anthrax and hydrophobia, while in constant conflict with the Medical Academy. Shunned and ridiculed by his colleagues, Pasteur moves with his wife (Josephine Hutchinson), and daughter, Annette (Anita Louise), to a small rural community, where he pursues the bacteria responsible for anthrax.

When the French government discovers that sheep from that

The Story of Louis Pasteur. With Josephine Hutchinson.

area do not suffer from the disease, Pasteur is once again placed at odds with the Medical Academy and, as usual, Dr. Charbonnet (Fritz Leiber) is his prime critic. A test is proposed, whereby twenty-five sheep will be vaccinated by Pasteur's serum and twenty-five others will remain untouched. The treated sheep are the only ones to

The Story of Louis Pasteur. With Henry O'Neill and Porter Hall.

The Story of Louis Pasteur. With Fritz Leiber and players.

survive and Pasteur is acclaimed by everyone except Charbonnet, who still isn't convinced about his microbe theory.

Next, Pasteur goes after a cure for hydrophobia. After years of research, he tries his unproven vaccine on a young boy, Joseph Meister (Dickie Moore), who has been bitten by a rabid dog. At the same time, Annette, married to her father's assistant, Jean Martel (Donald Woods), is expecting their first child. The only available physician is Charbonnet. He agrees to wash and sterilize his instruments prior to delivering the baby, only if Pasteur will renounce his claim to a cure for hydrophobia. Desperate, Pasteur agrees.

Young Joseph recovers and Charbonnet, as well as the French Medical Academy, finally acknowledge Pasteur's great contributions to mankind.

Pasteur was filmed under the working title, *Enemy of Man.* Even after the picture was finished, the studio was still not convinced that it was worth promoting. They initially sold it to exhibitors for a smaller percentage of the gross than usual. It opened at a second-run

The Story of Louis Pasteur. With C. Montague Shaw.

The Story of Louis Pasteur. With Leonid Snegoff.

theater in Chicago, and it was not until the reviews came out and word-of-mouth started building the box office that Warners realized what they had.

To prepare for his role, Muni read countless books on Pasteur, as well as other great scientists, such as Lister and Ehrlich. He even visited the Pasteur Institute outside of Paris. Aside from the Oscar, he was awarded the Volpi Cup by the International Cinema Exposition Committee in Venice, Italy.

Although parts of the picture today seem almost like a science lecture, the film as a whole is superb. Its major sequences are still engrossing to watch and the supporting performances are all first rate.

Muni and Fritz Leiber repeated their roles for Cecil B. DeMille's adaptation of *Pasteur,* which was heard on the "Lux Radio Theatre" over CBS on November 23, 1936.

In 1939, while riding his bicycle, Muni was bitten by a collie. The press found amusement in the fact that he *refused* the Pasteur treatment.

What the Critics Said

"Here is another splendid film, carefully and intelligently produced and credit all around. . . .

"Expert casting and splendid production are the points in the film's favor, primarily. Paul Muni in the title role is at his very top form and all the way down the other roles have been perfectly picked and handled."

Variety

". . . . we believe that Warners' *The Story of Louis Pasteur* is an excellent biography, just as it is a notable photoplay, dignified in subject, dramatic in treatment and brilliantly played by Paul Muni, Fritz Leiber, Josephine Hutchinson and many other members of the cast.

"Pasteur's life is warm and vital, of itself. It has lost none of that warmth through Mr. Muni's sensitive characterization, through the gifted direction of William Dieterle and the talents of a perfect cast. It may not be the province—and probably it was not the primary motive—of a Hollywood studio to create a film which is, at the same time, a monument to the life of a man. But *The Story of Louis Pasteur* is truly that."

New York Times

THE GOOD EARTH
(1937)

A Metro-Goldwyn-Mayer Picture. Produced by Irving G. Thalberg. Associate producer, Albert Lewin. Directed by Sidney Franklin. Based on the novel by Pearl S. Buck. Adapted for the stage by Owen and Donald Davis. Screenplay, Talbot Jennings, Tess Schlesinger, and Claudine West. Music Score, Herbert Stothart. Art Director, Cedric Gibbons. Photography, Karl Freund. Editor, Basil Wrangell. Photographed in Sepia. Released: February, 1937. 138 minutes.

Cast

Wang: Paul Muni; *O-lan:* Luise Rainer; *Uncle:* Walter Connolly; *Lotus:* Tillie Losch; *Cuckoo:* Jessie Ralph; *Old Father:* Charley Grapewin; *Elder Son:* Keye Luke; *Cousin:* Harold Huber; *Younger Son:* Roland Lui; *Old Mistress Aunt:* Soo Young; *Ching:* Chingwah Lee; *Gateman:* William Law; *Little Bride:* Mary Wong; *Banker:* Charles Middleton; *Little Fool:* Suzanna Kim; *Dancer:* Caroline Chew. *Also:* Chester Gan, Olaf Hytten, Miki Morita, Philip Ahn, Sammee Tong, and Richard Loo.

The Film

The Good Earth was another project that the studio head didn't want to do. This time, it was Metro-Goldwyn-Mayer's Louis B. Mayer who had to be convinced by producer Irving Thalberg. Said Mayer: "Who wants to see a picture about Chinese farmers?"

Thalberg argued that it was not a story about farmers, but a timeless saga of a man and his wife and the vicissitudes of their life together. He won over the mogul and was given a budget of $2,800,-000 for the production.

Once it was decided to use Caucasian actors for the principal roles in the film version of Pearl Buck's 1931 Pulitzer Prize-winning novel, Paul Muni seemed the only possible choice for the male lead, and Luise Rainer, the Academy Award winner in 1936 for her role in *The Great Ziegfeld,* was cast opposite him.

The drama tells the story of Wang Lung (Muni), a poor Chinese rice farmer, who marries O-Lan (Rainer), a kitchen slave he has never seen before. On their wedding night, the bride plants a discarded peach seed in their field.

With the help of his wife, Wang prospers. The couple has three children and, over the years, they acquire five more rice fields.

The Good Earth. With Roland Lui.

The Good Earth. With Luise Rainer.

The earth dries and famine comes to the northern part of China. Wang's uncle (Walter Connolly) implores him to sell his land, so he can feed his children. Wang refuses and, to stave off hunger, O-Lan feeds the family cooked earth.

Eventually, the family decides to go South with the other refugees and return to the farm when the famine is over. However, things are not much better in the city. O-Lan and the children must beg, since Wang has trouble finding work.

When revolution comes, O-Lan is swept by a mob that storms the palace. Knocked unconscious, she awakens to find a forgotten bag of priceless jewels close to her. Narrowly escaping a firing squad that is executing all looters, she brings the gems to her husband. The family returns home and buys the elegant Great House in the local village, along with all of its rich farmland.

Much time passes. Wang decides to take a teahouse dancer, Lotus (Tilly Losch), as his second wife. She, in turn, seduces Wang's youngest son (Roland Lui). When he discovers the betrayal, Wang beats his son.

The Good Earth. With Walter Connolly and Luise Rainer.

The Good Earth.

Locusts attack Wang's fields. His eldest son (Keye Luke), an agricultural college graduate, convinces Wang that this threat is not the "will of the gods," but an act of nature, which can be fought. Utilizing fire, water, shovels, gongs, hands, and feet to fight off the insects, Wang, his sons, and their workers save the crop.

O-Lan has been ill for some time and, on the night of her son's wedding, she dies. Wang realizes that all his hopes and successes

The Good Earth. With Charles Middleton and Walter Connolly.

would not have been possible, had it not been for her. As he looks at and feels the peach tree she planted on their wedding night, he says: "O-Lan, you are the earth."

The picture was shot in the San Fernando Valley and also utilized second-unit footage filmed in China. It took almost three years to complete.

The most memorable sequence in the production and one of the most spectacular scenes ever committed to film was the battle with the locusts. The crew that went to China shot the insects during their stay, and this material was intercut with close-ups of the locusts taken on a miniature stage back at the studio.

To prepare for his role, Muni spent four months in San Francisco's Chinatown, where he acquired his realistic walk and accent, which he used in the picture.

Muni was excellent in the film, but Luise Rainer stole the show. The part had a minimum of dialogue, requiring her to express her feelings through pantomime. She was magnificent and the performance earned her a second Oscar.

The Good Earth. With Charley Grapewin.

Irving Thalberg died before the production was completed and Louis B. Mayer dedicated the film to his memory.

The Good Earth was praised by the critics and became a financial success. Most film historians consider it one of the all-time cinema classics.

What the Critics Said

"More minute care and generous treatment has seldom been accorded a screenplay. The result is a true technical achievement with names enough to send it across.

"Paul Muni as Wang, with a great make-up, is a splendid lead for the film. Role is something any actor would relish, for it's the kind that gives credit for restraint and pays off automatically on just looking the part regardless of performance."

Variety

"Once again Metro-Goldwyn-Mayer has enriched the screen with a superb translation of a literary classic. Its film of Pearl Buck's *The Good Earth,* which had its premiere at the Astor Theatre last night, is one of the finest things Hollywood has done this season or any other. . . . The performances, direction and photography are of uniform excellence, and have been fused perfectly into a dignified, beautiful and soberly dramatic production.

". . . Paul Muni, flawless in the early sequences, seemed to me to step out of his Chinese character in the post-famine episodes, talking, walking, reacting more as Muni than as Wang Lung.

". . . The picture does full justice to the novel, and that is the highest praise one can give it."

New York Times

THE WOMAN I LOVE
(1937)

An RKO-Radio Release of an Albert Lewis Production. Directed by Anatole Litvak. Screenplay by Mary Borden from the French film, *L'Equipage,* and novel of the same name by Joseph Kessel. Score, Arthur Honneger and Maurice Thiriet. Camera, Charles Rosher. Special Effects, Vernon Walker. Editor, Henri Rust. Original title: *Escadrille.* Released: April, 1937. 85 minutes.

Cast

Maury: Paul Muni; *Denise:* Miriam Hopkins; *Jean:* Louis Hayward; *Captain:* Colin Clive; *Deschamps:* Minor Watson; *Mother:* Elizabeth Risdon; *Berthier:* Paul Guilfoyle; *Georges:* Wally Albright; *Florence:* Mady Christians; *Doctor:* Alec Craig; *Mezzioves:* Owen Davis Jr.; *Duprez:* Sterling Holloway; *Mathieu:* Vince Barnett.

The Woman I Love. With Louis Hayward.

The Film

RKO initially wanted Charles Boyer for this World War I air/action drama, which was based on a 1927 French film, *L'Equipage*. When Boyer refused the project, producer Albert Lewis suggested Paul Muni, who liked the story and agreed to do the film if Jack Warner would agree to loan him to the other studio. After much negotiation, terms were reached with Warner Brothers.

The picture was one of Muni's lesser efforts in all respects. His role of Maury, the Lafayette Escadrille pilot with a reputation of being a jinx, is actually a secondary one.

Many of Maury's men have been killed in recent air battles and the other men in his squadron feel that he is "unlucky" to fly with. His one friend is Jean (Louis Hayward), a young pilot, who subsequently falls in love and has an affair with Maury's wife, Denise (Miriam Hopkins). The story has the usual clichés of most "triangle" films with the result, in this case, that Maury is injured in a tense air battle, in which Jean is killed. Denise nurses Maury back

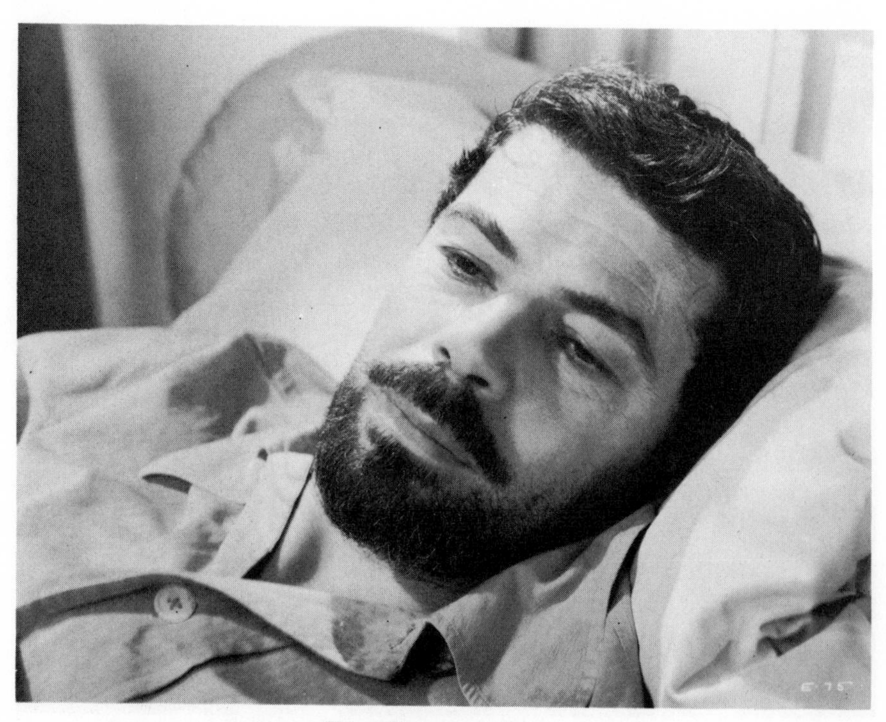

The Woman I Love.

The Woman I Love. With Owen Davis, Jr., Miriam Hopkins, and players.

The Woman I Love. With Louis Hayward.

The Woman I Love. With Miriam Hopkins.

to health and asks his forgiveness for her betrayal.

The Woman I Love, originally titled *Escadrille,* was the first film directed by Anatole Litvak in this country. The picture, distinguished only by some well-staged flying sequences, did nothing to further the careers of anyone involved and, today, is virtually forgotten.

What the Critics Said

"A thrill air picture plus a down-to-earth love story. But the love angle is too typically French to convince the average American femme. Latter is likely to find the yarn hard to believe despite being sympathetic. On top of that, picture has one of those unsatisfactory endings which may annoy the girls no end.

". . . All three leads are very good, with Hayward, perhaps, getting the break because of the story."

Variety

"It was directed by Anatole Litvak, which should have recommended it, but does not; and it has been played with competence—

scarcely more—by Paul Muni, Miriam Hopkins and Louis Hayward.

"Somehow the film gives the impression of being ever so out of focus. Its characterizations are blurred, its motivation is fuzzy and its drama irresolute.

". . . Mr. Muni's role is strangely unsympathetic. His Pasteur-like beard, his stoop and shambling gait are as unmilitary as they are unromantic."

New York Times

THE LIFE OF EMILE ZOLA
(1937)

A Warner Brothers Production and release. Production Supervisor, Henry Blanke. Directed by William Dieterle. Story, Heinz Herald and Geza Herczeg. Screenplay, Heinz Herald, Geza Herczeg, and Norman Reilly Raine. Music, Max Steiner. Cinematography, Tony Gaudio. Editor, Warren Lowe. Art Director, Anton Grot. Makeup, Perc Westmore. Dialogue Director, Irving Rapper. Gowns, Milo Anderson and Ali Hubert. Released: July, 1937. 116 minutes.

Cast

Emile Zola: Paul Muni; *Lucie Dreyfus:* Gale Sondergaard; *Captain Alfred Dreyfus:* Joseph Schildkraut; *Alexandrine Zola:* Gloria Holden; *Maitre Labori:* Donald Crisp; *Nana:* Erin O'Brien-Moore; *Charpentier:* John Litel; *Colonel Picquart:* Henry O'Neill; *Anatole France:* Morris Carnovsky; *Major Dort:* Louis Calhern; *Commander of Paris:* Ralph Morgan; *Major Walsin-Esterhazy:* Robert Barrat; *Paul Cezanne:* Vladimir Sokoloff; *Chief of Staff:* Harry Davenport; *Major Henry:* Robert Warwick; *M. Delagorgue:* Charles Richman; *Pierre Dreyfus:* Dickie Moore; *Jeanne Dreyfus:* Rolla Gourvitch; *Minister of War:* Gilbert Emery; *Colonel Sandherr:* Walter Kingsford; *Asst. Chief of Staff:* Paul Everton; *Cavaignac:* Montagu Love; *Van Cassell:* Frank Sheridan; *Mr. Richards:* Lumsden Hare; *Helen Richards:* Marcia Mae Jones; *Madame Zola:* Florence Roberts; *Georges Clemenceau:* Grant Mitchell; *Captain Guignet:* Moroni Olsen; *Brucker:* Egon Brecher. *Also:* Frank Reicher, Walter O. Stahl, Frank Darien, Countess Iphigenie Castiglioni, Arthur Aylesworth, Frank Mayo, Alexander Leftwich, Paul Irving, Pierre Watkin, and Holmes Herbert.

The Film

With *The Life of Emile Zola,* Paul Muni reached the pinnacle of his career. The project was Warner Brothers' prestige follow-up to *Louis Pasteur* and they billed their star as "*Mr.* Paul Muni" with emphasis on the "Mister." It was the most highly praised film of 1937, taking the Academy Award for Best Picture, with Muni being nominated a fourth time for Best Actor, as well as winning that honor from the New York Film Critics. Joseph Schildkraut won the Best Supporting Actor Oscar for his performance.

The screenplay had originally been sent to Ernst Lubitsch at Paramount, who liked the project, but suggested to the agent that he take it to his friend, Henry Blanke, at Warners. Said Lubitsch: "I don't have an actor that can play this role. Blanke has Muni."

The picture was Muni's second experience with the story of Dreyfus. In 1924, he had done a production of Romain Rolland's *Wolves* with Maurice Schwartz in the Yiddish Art Theatre. The three-act play was a symbolic treatment of the Dreyfus case, with Muni doing the role of the defendant.

The film begins with Zola (Muni) as a struggling young writer living in a cold attic with Paul Cezanne (Vladimir Sokoloff). They are visited by Emile's fiancée (Gloria Holden) and mother (Florence Roberts).

Zola's books, dealing with social injustices in France, have not been well received by the public or the government. He achieves his first major success after he meets a young prostitute (Erin O'Brien-

The Life of Emile Zola. Vladimir Sokoloff, Muni, Erin O'Brien-Moore, and player.

Moore) and writes a book based on her plight. The result is *Nana* and, although termed "scandalous," it becomes the best-selling novel of the day.

The years pass. Zola is recognized as France's greatest novelist. His works deal with social hypocrisy and injustice, striving for truth and freedom.

One evening, he is visited by Lucie Dreyfus (Gale Sondergaard), wife of Captain Alfred Dreyfus (Joseph Schildkraut), a French Army officer, who is serving a life term on Devil's Island for treason.

Actually, the traitor is Major Walsin-Esterhazy (Robert Barrat). Not knowing the identity of the guilty party at the time, the army needed a scapegoat and Dreyfus was chosen by the high command to be "tried," convicted, dishonorably discharged, and sent to the island prison. Later, when the true facts were learned, the military officers were too embarrassed to correct their "error" and acquitted Esterhazy in a "mock" court-martial.

Zola, with the support of his friends, Anatole France (Morris Carnovsky) and legal counsel Maitre Labori (Donald Crisp), takes up Dreyfus's cause. He publishes an editorial, "I Accuse," which relates the scandal behind the entire affair. The army brings him to

The Life of Emile Zola. With players.

trial for libel and, in a prejudiced courtroom, full of army officers calling him "traitor," the writer is convicted.

Rather than go to prison, Zola flees to London, where he continues to write on Dreyfus's behalf. Finally, after much public pressure is brought to bear, the French government investigates the matter. The truth is found out: the guilty officers are punished; Dreyfus is pardoned; and Zola is allowed to return home.

The Life of Emile Zola.

The Life of Emile Zola. With Gale Sondergaard.

The Life of Emile Zola. Donald Crisp, Grant Mitchell, Muni, and Gloria Holden.

The Life of Emile Zola. With Donald Crisp and John Litel.

The Life of Emile Zola. With Donald Crisp.

However, Zola dies before he can meet Dreyfus and, at the funeral, Anatole France describes him as "a moment in the conscience of Man."

To prepare for his role, Muni read all of Zola's major works, went over accounts of his life and of the Dreyfus case, studied portraits, then experimented with various makeups, gestures, and personal habits.

In an interview with the *Los Angeles Times* given at the time of the film's release, the actor said: "I feel that today, perhaps more than ever before, we need such films. *Zola* is positive proof that Hollywood can produce an intelligent, serious picture that is also a box-office success. Of course, it's going against all of the rules. No sex! Or perhaps *Zola* is one of the sexiest pictures ever filmed, since it's about men and women."

On May 8, 1939, Muni and Josephine Hutchinson did *Zola* for Cecil B. DeMille's "Lux Radio Theatre" over CBS.

Warner Brothers produced the picture not expecting it to be a

The Life of Emile Zola. Muni is center. Players include: Donald Crisp, Grant Mitchell, Gale Sondergaard, John Litel, and Gloria Holden.

financial success, however they were happily mistaken in this assessment.

What the Critics Said

"Warner's most ambitious film production of many months, *The Life of Emile Zola,* is a vibrant, tense and emotional story about the man who fought a nation with his pen and successfully championed the cause of the exiled Capt. Alfred Dreyfus. With Paul Muni in the title role, supported by distinguished players in sustaining parts, the film is destined to box-office approval of the most substantial character. It is finely made and merits high rating as cinema art and significant recognition as major showmanship.

"The picture is Muni's all the way, even when he is off screen."

Variety

"Rich, dignified, honest and strong, it is at once the finest historical film ever made and the greatest screen biography, greater even than *The Story of Louis Pasteur*. . . .

"Like *Pasteur,* the picture has captured the spirit of a man and his times; unlike *Pasteur*—and this is the factor which gives it preeminence—it has followed not merely the spirit but, to a rare degree, the very letter of his life and of the historically significant lives about him. And, still more miraculously, it has achieved this brilliant end without self-consciousness, without strutting glorification, without throwing history out of focus to build up the importance of its central figure.

"Paul Muni's portrayal of Zola is, without doubt, the best thing he has done. Fiery, bitter, compassionate as the young novelist; settled, complacent, content to rest from the wars in his later years; then forced into the struggle again, although he resisted it, when the Dreyfus case whispered to his conscience—Mr. Muni has given us a human and well-rounded portrait."

New York Times

JUAREZ
(1939)

A Warner Brothers Production and release. Produced by Hal B. Wallis. Directed by William Dieterle. Based on the play *Juarez and Maximilian* by Franz Werfel and the novel *The Phantom Crown* by Bertita Harding. Associate Producer, Henry Blanke. Screenplay, John Huston, Wolfgang Reinhardt, Aeneas MacKenzie. Art Director, Anton Grot. Music, Erich Wolfgang Korngold. Musical Director, Leo F. Forbstein. Cameraman, Tony Gaudio. Editor, Warren Low. Released: April, 1939. 132 minutes.

Cast

Benito Pablo Juarez: Paul Muni; *Empress Carlota von Habsburg:* Bette Davis; *Emperor Maximilian von Habsburg:* Brian Aherne; *Louis Napoleon:* Claude Rains; *Porfirio Diaz:* John Garfield; *Marechal Bazaine:* Donald Crisp; *Empress Eugenie:* Gale Sondergaard; *Alejandro Uradi:* Joseph Calleia; *Colonel Miguel Lopez:* Gilbert Roland; *Miguel Miramon:* Henry O'Neill; *Riva Palacio:* Pedro de Cordoba; *Jose de Montares:* Montagu Love; *Dr. Samuel Basch:* Harry Davenport; *Achille Fould:* Walter Fenner; *Drouyn de Lhuys:* Alex Leftwich; *Major DuPont:* Robert Warwick; *Mariano Escobedo:* John Miljan; *Carbajal:* Irving Pichel; *Prince Metternich:* Walter Kingsford; *Lerdo de Tejada:* Monte Blue; *LeMarc:* Louis Calhern; *Camilo:* Vladimir Sokoloff; *Countess Battenberg:* Georgia Caine. *Also:* Gennaro Curci, Bill Wilkerson, Hugh Sothern, Fred Malatesta, Carlos de Valdez, Frank Lackteen, Walter O. Stahl, Frank Reicher, Holmes Herbert, Egon Brecher, Manuel Diaz, Mickey Kuhn, Lillian Nicholson, Noble Johnson, and Grant Mitchell.

The Film

Released in 1939, this historical drama had Muni, dressed in a Prince Albert and a stovepipe hat, playing Benito Pablo Juarez, the idealistic Indian, who overcame a foreign, European dictatorship during the last century and established a democracy in Mexico. The film was based, in part, on a play, *Juarez and Maximilian* by Franz Werfel, and a book, *The Phantom Crown* by Bertita Harding.

The narrative begins with Napoleon III of France (Claude Rains) appointing Maximilian von Habsburg (Brian Aherne), the archduke of Austria, as emperor of Mexico. When Maximilian and

Juarez. With John Miljan.

his wife, Carlota (Bette Davis), arrive in Vera Cruz, they are met with opposition from the Mexican people, who are against French rule. Leader in the fight is the country's president, Benito Juarez, currently in hiding with his various aides, including Porfirio Diaz (John Garfield).

Maximilian refuses to sign edicts that would take land from the Mexican peons and return it to wealthy statesmen. In an effort to achieve peace with the Juarez forces, he offers to make the exiled president his secretary of state. Juarez answers the proposal by having a French munitions cache destroyed on the day that the emperor and his wife, as a sign of good faith, adopt a Mexican child.

Angered by this "slap," Maximilian signs a decree calling for the execution of anyone committing an act of aggression against French authority. He later realizes that this dictate was a mistake and he is, in fact, merely a pawn in a political war. Under the terms of the Monroe Doctrine, the United States supports the Juarez cause and formally requests Napoleon to withdraw his forces from Mexico.

Carlota goes to France to plead with Napoleon to help Maximilian, who, as a matter of honor, refuses to flee. She is refused and, subsequently, has a mental collapse.

Maximilian is captured and executed by the Mexican forces. Again in power, Juarez pays tribute to the late emperor, who he realizes was a dedicated leader.

Prior to start of production, Muni and director William Dieterle made a six-week tour of Mexico, visiting every place a new fact on Benito Juarez and his record of accomplishments could be learned. The research department of Warner Brothers also supplied the pair with 372 books, documents, pieces of correspondence, and albums of rare photographs.

Associate producer Henry Blanke recalls the picture: "We made our mistake by dividing the action between Juarez and the Maximilian/Carlota relationship. If we had followed the Franz Werfel play more closely, we would have had a much stronger film. Juarez never appears in the play."

Since the antagonists never meet, *Juarez* was virtually shot as two separate pictures, with the Maximilian/Carlota scenes going before the cameras first. Muni viewed the already edited footage, then pre-

Juarez. Joseph Calleia, John Garfield, John Miljan, Muni.

Juarez. With Monte Blue.

Juarez.

sented the producers with several more pages of dialogue that he wanted added to his role. Since he was then the most important star on the Warner lot, his request was granted.

The final picture was far too long and the editing was, unfortunately, done on the Maximilian/Carlota scenes, which were the strongest in the production. The result was an interesting film from the standpoint of a "documentary," but one with little dramatic focus. In general, performances were excellent. Muni was restrained in comparison to his previous work. Reviews were mixed and the project was not financially successful.

Like many Warner Brothers historical pictures of the period, such as *Zola* and Errol Flynn's *The Sea Hawk,* the patriotic speeches in *Juarez* seem to have a double edge to them. When Muni talks of European countries invading the lands of simple people, it's as if he were directing his remarks toward the events that were then taking place in Nazi Germany.

Juarez.

What the Critics Said

"To the list of distinguished characters whom he has created in films, Paul Muni now adds a portrait of Benito Pablo Juarez, Mexican patriot and liberator. With the aid of Bette Davis, co-starring in the tragic role of Carlota, of Brian Aherne giving an excellent performance as the ill-fated Maximilian, and a story that points up the parallels of conflicting political thought of today and three-quarters of a century ago, Muni again commands attention from the trade and public in a documentary picture. It's among the best that has been produced by Warners."

Variety

"Ideologically the new Warner film is faultless. What it has to say about the conflict between imperialist, benevolent despot and democrat has been expressed logically and eloquently, with reasonable fidelity to historic fact, through the speeches and performance of Paul Muni, Brian Aherne, Claude Rains, John Garfield and other members of a richly endowed cast.

". . . *Juarez* has not been smoothly assembled. Its central character has been thrown out of focus by a lesser one. Too much and too little attention has been paid to the subordinate people in the drama. . . . The picture runs for something more than two hours, which should have been enough to balance its budget and its plot. Yet it is out of balance, in character and in narrative. Possibly the fault is in the editing, although that would not explain it all.

"Juarez clearly is the hero of history, but Maximilian is the hero of the picture. Perhaps this was inevitable by the very nature of the men. For Mr. Muni's performance of Juarez, however brilliant, is restricted by the range of the character itself and Juarez was a stoic. It is impossible to portray a symbol—as the Zapotecan was—with anything but austerity.

". . . *Juarez,* with all its faults, still must be rated a distinguished, memorable and socially valuable film."

New York Times

WE ARE NOT ALONE
(1939)

A Warner Brothers Release of a Henry Blanke Production. Executive Producer, Hal B. Wallis. Directed by Edmund Goulding. Screenplay, James Hilton and Milton Krims from a novel by Hilton. Music, Max Steiner. Cameraman, Tony Gaudio. Editor, Warren Low. Special Effects, Byron Haskin and H. F. Koenekamp. Released: November, 1939. 112 minutes.

Cast

Dr. David Newcome: Paul Muni; *Leni:* Jane Bryan; *Jessica:* Flora Robson; *Gerald:* Raymond Severn; *Susan:* Una O'Connor; *Dawson:* Henry Daniell; *Major Millman:* Montagu Love; *Sr. Wm. Clintock:* James Stephenson; *Sr. Guy Lockwood:* Stanley Logan; *Judge:* Cecil Kellaway. *Also:* Alan Napier, Ely Malyon, Douglas Scott, Crawford Kent, May Beatty, and Billy Bevan.

The Film

Due to his insecurity about playing romantic roles, Muni was initially reluctant to accept the part of Dr. David Newcome in the film version of James Hilton's novel. It was his wife, Bella, who altered his thinking.

The actor insisted that Hilton be called in to rewrite the screenplay. After reading the novelist's draft, Muni commented: "That's the difference between chicken shit and chicken salad!"

The story, set in 1914, dealt with Dr. Newcome, a gentle, provincial English physician, married to a shrewish wife, Jessica (Flora Robson). The couple have a high-strung, imaginative son, Gerald (Raymond Severn), whose nervousness is aggravated by his mother's harsh nature.

Newcome treats a lonely young Austrian dancer, Leni (Jane Bryan), for a broken wrist and, again later, after she attempts suicide. He sympathizes with her problems and finds her a place to stay until she can gain employment.

In order to get Gerald away from his mother's badgering, Newcome takes his son with him when he goes to work and leaves the lad with Leni while he visits patients. Leni and Gerald like each other immediately. After a conference with Jessica, the young woman is hired as the boy's governess.

We Are Not Alone. Jane Bryan, Muni, Flora Robson, and Una O'Connor.

We Are Not Alone. With Jane Bryan.

We Are Not Alone. With Stanley Logan.

When Jessica learns that Leni is a former dancer and had attempted suicide, she insists that she be discharged and sends Gerald away to stay with her pious brother, the Archdeacon of Calderbury.

Furious at his wife, Newcome does not realize that he is in love with Leni, who, with his help, enters a musical school not far away.

Gerald sneaks back home to see Leni. While searching for a pocketknife his mother had taken from him, he accidently knocks over and breaks several of his father's medicine bottles. In a panic, the boys stuffs the pills back into the bottles, not realizing that the labels are now incorrect.

World War I breaks out and the townsfolk are driven into a frenzy. Mobs smash the windows of shops owned by Germans and shout angry threats. Because she is Austrian, Newcome realizes the potential danger to Leni and takes her to a nearby town, where he can put her on a train for the first leg of a journey back to her homeland.

Meanwhile, Jessica, suffering a headache, takes some tablets from

We Are Not Alone. With Jane Bryan.

one of the Doctor's medicine bottles. She dies, the victim of the poison pills Gerald had innocently placed in the wrong bottle.

Newcome and Leni are arrested and tried for murder. Against them is the appearance of flight and the fact that the doctor cannot explain how the poison pills got into the wrong bottle. Gerald, the only person that could explain the situation, knows nothing of what happened, as his father had insisted he be "protected."

We Are Not Alone. With Montagu Love, Alan Napier, and players.

Under oath, Newcome admits, to his own surprise, that he loves Leni. This seals their fate. They are found guilty and sentenced to hang.

On the night before their execution, Newcome and Leni are allowed a few moments alone together. They profess their love for each other and the doctor tells her that Death is not to be feared. He is an old friend, who takes the hardest cases and solves them happily.

The couple go to the gallows, knowing they will meet again in a better world.

Actress Dolly Haass had originally been cast as Leni. However, there was an immediate personality conflict between her and Muni. After three weeks of filming, he insisted she be replaced. Overnight, Warner contract player Jane Bryan was called in by director Edmund Goulding to test with Muni. Twenty-four hours later, she knew she had the part.

Jane Bryan, now Mrs. Justin Dart, recalls the picture: "There was a very tense atmosphere on the set. We'd finish doing a scene that was set at the start of the First World War, then, after the director called 'Cut!,' go over to the radio and listen to the current war news from Europe, which paralleled the film we were doing.

"Muni was very tender in our scenes together. He seemed to say it all with his eyes."

The script called for Newcome to play the violin in the picture. Muni had studied the instrument for years and the music heard from the screen was his own . . . recorded as he played.

Although critics around the country gave it excellent notices, *We Are Not Alone* "bombed" at the box office. Possibly, it was the film's downbeat ending that kept audiences away.

The picture was Muni's tenth and final one for Warner Brothers.

What the Critics Said

"An interesting study, as well as satisfying entertainment . . . handsomely produced, skillfully directed and eloquently played.

"Looking something like a younger Fritz Kreisler and playing slightly in the manner of Ronald Colman, Muni seems completely the suburban English physician. He not only achieves the necessary

We Are Not Alone. With Raymond Severn.

light touch in the part, but he has dropped the mannerisms with which he adorned such character parts as Zola, Juarez and others. It is a stirring performance, direct and subtle."

Variety

". . . *We Are Not Alone* emerges as a film of rare tenderness and beauty, compassionate and grave, possessed of all the quality of serenity. Mr. Hilton, we repeat, does not write for the screen; but the screen has found in his writings a vast store of the one substance it so greatly needs: humanity.

"Paul Muni's performance of the little doctor, Jane Bryan's as Leni, Flora Robson's as the wife are a piece in their perfection. Of Mr. Muni it was to be expected. His grasp of the role has been sure and right; there is no flaw in it.

". . . it must be counted one of the best films of the year."

New York Times

HUDSON'S BAY
(1940)

A Twentieth Century-Fox Release of a Kenneth Macgowan Production. Directed by Irving Pichel. Original Screenplay, Lamar Trotti. Camera, Peverell Marley and George Barnes. Technical Advisor, Clifford Wilson. Music, Alfred Newman. Editor, Robert Simpson. Released: December, 1940. 94 minutes.

Cast

Pierre Radisson: Paul Muni; *Barbara Hall:* Gene Tierney; *Gooseberry:* Laird Cregar; *Lord Edward Crew:* John Sutton; *Nell Gwynn:* Virginia Field; *King Charles:* Vincent Price; *Prince Rupert:* Nigel Bruce; *Governor d'Argenson:* Montagu Love; *Gerald Hall:* Morton Lowry. *Also:* Robert Greig, Lumsden Hare, Chief Thundercloud, Lionel Pape, Florence Bates, Ian Wolfe, and Chief John Big Tree.

The Film

Aside from the fact that it gave him the chance to interpret another historical character, Muni's main reason for doing *Hudson's Bay* was that it was the first opportunity he'd ever had to play an adventurous role in contrast to his former more serious parts.

Here, he was Pierre Radisson, the French-Canadian trapper of the seventeenth century, who sold King Charles II the idea of forming the Hudson's Bay Company.

Radisson and his partner, Gooseberry (Laird Cregar) meet and befriend Lord Edward Crew (John Sutton), a British nobleman, who has been exiled to Canada. After months of trapping and trading with the Indians, the trio sails to England to present to King Charles (Vincent Price) the idea for the Hudson's Bay Trading Company. Radisson paints the monarch a picture of the great monetary gains that can be achieved for England by such a venture. Charles is convinced, the financing for the expedition secured, and Radisson, Gooseberry and Crew return to Canada, taking along with them Sir Gerald Hall (Morton Lowry), brother of Barbara Hall (Gene Tierney), Crew's fiancée.

The trading post is established and activities go along smoothly until Sir Gerald, a weakling and coward, causes the death of an Indian due to his drunkeness. The Indian chief threatens to kill everyone on the post, unless the man responsible for the death is

Hudson's Bay. With Gene Tierney and John Sutton.

Hudson's Bay. With John Sutton and Morton Lowry.

punished. In order to avert a war, Radisson, over Crew's violent objections, has Sir Gerald executed by a firing squad.

When the successful trio of fur traders return to England, Charles has them arrested for the murder of Gerald. They escape and force their way into the king's court. Radisson informs Charles that *he* is the only one that the Indians will cooperate with and, if he is executed, that will be the end of the Hudson's Bay Company. The king submits. Radisson and Gooseberry go back to Canada, while Lord Crew marries Barbara.

Two years of research and planning preceded actual production on the picture. When filming began, it was in the wilds of Idaho, where the terrain resembled primitive Hudson's Bay district as it was in the seventeenth century. The company was on location for three weeks, then returned to the studio to finish.

Muni was completely inexperienced with canoes. While doing a scene on the backlot lake, he lost his balance and tumbled into seven feet of water. A bad cold developed and the actor was forced to stay home a few days while director Irving Pichel shot around him.

Hudson's Bay. With Laird Cregar and John Sutton.

Hudson's Bay. With John Sutton and Laird Cregar.

The completed picture's major problem was a talky screenplay with very little action. Muni was entertaining to watch, but, unfortunately, director Pichel was unable to curb his tendency to "overplay" in certain scenes. The strongest performance was given by Laird Cregar, doing his second film.

What the Critics Said

"Zanuck takes another sideswipe at history here and comes off second best again. The story of the birth of the Hudson's Bay Company, in the heart of Canada, has a good deal of intrinsic and automatic excitement, but it is played for chatter-chatter here with Paul Muni declaiming long speech after long speech to slow up and reduce to a minimum the little action that there is in the first place.

". . . Muni must have smiled with pleasure when he first read the script and contemplated the role. It permits him to strut his stuff in typical Muni fashion. It has long declamations galore, even if they

Hudson's Bay. With John Sutton.

are of the 'Canada—She my wife—no woman—joost Canada' school of writing."

Variety

". . . Their [Fox's] Hudson's Bay is as static and ponderous as a bale of furs, and the only breath it is filled with is that which the characters expend in endless talk.

". . . Radisson is, of course, Mr. Muni with a coonskin hat, beard and accent, which is thicker than the hair on his head. . . ."

New York Times

"Muni makes Radisson a living being. The role is one susceptible to an infinity of subtle shadings of which he takes the full advantage to be expected of him."

Hollywood Reporter

THE COMMANDOS STRIKE AT DAWN
(1942)

A Columbia Release of a Lester Cowan Production. Directed by John Farrow. Screenplay by Irwin Shaw. Story, C. S. Forester. Photography, William C. Mellor. Musical Score, Louis Gruenberg. Musical Director, M. W. Stoloff. Editor, Anne Bauchens. Art Director, Edward Jewell. Released: December, 1942. 96 minutes.

Cast

Eric Toresen: Paul Muni; *Judith Bowen:* Anna Lee; *Mrs. Bergesen:* Lillian Gish; *Admiral Bowen:* Sir Cedric Hardwicke; *Robert Bowen:* Robert Coote; *Bergesen:* Ray Collins; *Hilma Arnesen:* Rosemary DeCamp; *German Captain:* Alexander Knox; *Anna Korstad:* Elisabeth Fraser; *Gunner Korstad:* Richard Derr; *Johan Garmo:* Erville Alderson; *Pastor:* Rod Cameron; *Karl Arnesen:* Louis Jean Heydt; *School Teacher:* George Macready. *Also:* Ann Carter, Barbara Everest, Arthur Margetson, Captain V. S. Godfrey, RCN, Commander C. M. Cree, RCN, Brigadier R. A. Fraser, CRA, Commander C. T. Beard, RCN, Sergeant-Major L. E. Kemp, CRA, Sergeant-Major Mickey Miquelon, CRA.

The Film

After two years away from the screen, Muni returned in 1942 to make a realistic war drama for Columbia, which depicted Norwegian sabotage and rebellion against the Nazi forces.

He was cast as Eric Toreson, a widower, who lives with his young daughter (Ann Carter) in a small village on the coast of Norway. Prior to the Nazi invasion, he has a brief romance with Judith Bowen (Anna Lee), who is visiting the country with her father, a British Admiral (Sir Cedric Hardwicke).

Shortly thereafter, a regiment of German soldiers, led by a captain (Alexander Knox), occupies the village. Toreson and some other male villagers escape and make their way in a small boat to England. Toreson agrees to lead a troop of British commandos back to Norway to destroy a German airfield that he had accidentally discovered and also to rescue his daughter.

The raid against the airfield is successful, but Toreson learns that the Nazis have discovered his daughter's hiding place and are holding her hostage in the village. The commandos attack the village and Toreson is killed. His daughter, however, is rescued and taken back to England.

To find a suitable substitute for the Norwegian terrain, the production company traveled to Vancouver Island in British Columbia. The project received extensive help from the Royal Canadian Navy, Royal Canadian Air Force, and Royal Air Force. Technical directors were underground warfare experts from Canada's Norwegian Flying School, all of whom had fled from their occupied homeland.

John Farrow, of *Wake Island* fame, directed the picture. Muni was excellent, although his role was not a demanding one. The film, viewed today, is still exciting and its propaganda aspects do not detract.

What the Critics Said

"No mere grandiose battle melodrama suspended upon fierce excitement is this account of tough British Commandos in action. Excitement it has, and the deadly in-fighting of new tactics, to create breathless suspense. But beyond these elements in the screenplay and

Commandos Strike at Dawn. With Robert Coote.

Commandos Strike at Dawn. Player, Muni, and Ray Collins.

Commandos Strike at Dawn. With Robert Coote.

Commandos Strike at Dawn. Barbara Everest, Ann Carter, Muni.

Commandos Strike at Dawn.

Commandos Strike at Dawn. With Cedric Hardwicke and Anna Lee.

its treatment of the big issues of the war, told and performed with powerful dramatic fervor and scope, against the German invasion and ravishment of Norway. And for all its ferocious combat and such grim avenging justice as seldom has been shown on the lately timid American screen, *Commandos Strike at Dawn* is exalting, rather than depressive. It builds up a terrific charge of emotion, but it also is permitted to discharge that audience emotion with a terrific purge. *Commandos* will be greatly relished by audiences for its substance and its fine craftsmanship, dealt out with keen showmanship.

". . . Paul Muni delivers a strong and persuasive characterization as the Norwegian meteorologist and patriot, who dies in a final charge of the Commandos he has led back to his homeland as they rescue his little daughter, Ann Carter, and a group of hostages."

Variety

"Subordinating performance honors to the betterment of the film results in a group of enormously effective portrayals. Paul Muni is one especially to benefit from this technique. He is a leader among the kind gentle people of a Norwegian village and is the first to awaken to the necessity of 'resisting' the Nazi invasion."

Hollywood Reporter

". . . whatever the faults of the picture—however stagey parts of it may be and in spite of an incidental romance which demands somewhat embarrassing things of him—the fact is quite clearly apparent that Mr. Muni had had his heart and soul in it and that its most affecting moments are largely due to him."

New York Times

STAGE DOOR CANTEEN
(1943)

A Sol Lesser Production. Released thru United Artists. Directed by Frank Borzage. Associate Producer, Barnett Briskin. Screenplay, Delmer Daves. Photography, Harry Wild. Art Director, Hans Peters. Editor, Hal Kern. Sound, Hugh McDonald. Musical Score, Freddie Rich. Released: May, 1943. 132 minutes.

Cast

Eileen: Cheryl Walker; *"Dakota":* William Terry; *Jean:* Marjorie Riordan; *"California":* Lon McCallister; *Ella Sue:* Margaret Early; *"Texas":* Michael Harrison; *Mamie:* Dorothea Kent; *"Jersey":* Fred Brady; *Lillian:* Marion Shockley; *The Australian:* Patrick O'Moore; *Girl:* Ruth Roman. *Guest Stars:* Judith Anderson, Henry Armetta, Benny Baker, Kenny Baker, Tallulah Bankhead, Ralph Bellamy, Edgar Bergen and Charlie McCarthy, Ray Bolger, Helen Broderick, Ina Claire, Katharine Cornell, Lloyd Corrigan, Jane Cowl, Jane Darwell, William Demarest, Virginia Field, Dorothy Fields, Gracie Fields, Lynn Fontanne, Arlene Francis, Vinton Freedley, Billy Gilbert, Lucile Gleason, Vera Gordon, Virginia Grey, Helen Hayes, Katharine Hepburn, Hugh Herbert, Jean Hersholt, Sam Jaffe, Allen Jenkins, George Jessel, Roscoe Karns, Virginia Kaye, Tom Kennedy, Otto Kruger, June Lang, Betty Lawford, Gertrude Lawrence, Gypsy Rose Lee, Alfred Lunt, Bert Lytell, Harpo Marx, Aline MacMahon, Elsa Maxwell, Helen Menken, Yehudi Menuhin, Ethel Merman, Ralph Morgan, Alan Mowbray, Paul Muni, Elliott Nugent, Merle Oberon, Franklin Pangborn, Helen Parrish, Brock Pemberton, George Raft, Lanny Ross, Selena Royle, Martha Scott, Cornelia Otis Skinner, Ned Sparks, Bill Stern, Ethel Waters, Johnny Weissmuller, Arleen Whelan, Dame May Whitty, Ed Wynn. *And:* Count Basie and His Band, Xavier Cugat and His Orchestra, with Lina Romay, Benny Goodman and His Orchestra, with Peggy Lee, Kay Kyser and His Band, Freddy Martin and His Orchestra, Guy Lombardo and His Orchestra.

The Film

This 1943 film had sixty-five stars in its cast . . . all playing themselves. They were attracted by the fact that eighty percent of the picture's profits were to go to the canteens operated by the American Theatre Wing.

Stage Door Canteen. With Cheryl Walker and Marjorie Riordan.

The story dealt with Eileen (Cheryl Walker), an ambitious actress, who becomes a junior hostess at the New York Stage Door Canteen. There she meets Private Ed "Dakota" Smith (William Terry), who is soon to be shipped to the war zone. They don't get along well at first, but after a couple of days, discover that they are in love. They plan to marry the next evening.

Eileen goes to the Canteen to meet "Dakota," but is informed by an Australian soldier that he was shipped out that morning. Katharine Hepburn consoles her and gives her the strength to continue doing her important morale work at the Canteen until "Dakota" returns.

Muni appeared as himself in one brief sequence, which takes place in a theater close to the Canteen. Eileen has been cast in Muni's new play and he meets her backstage to offer congratulations.

Stage Door Canteen received two Academy Award nominations: Best Song ("We Mustn't Say Goodbye" by Al Dubin and Jimmy Monaco) and Best Scoring of a Musical Picture (Frederic E. Rich). It was recut and reissued in 1949 with an updated commentary.

What the Critics Said

"Its triple love story—uniformed boy meets Canteen girl—garnished by the characteristic outpourings of nearly 100 top names of the entertainment world, *Stage Door Canteen* in film emerges as a lavish and unqualified piece of entertainment for mass and class patronage. It tops the showmanship career of Sol Lesser with an important and elegant production, which performs a public service while supplying one of the major offerings of the year. . . ."

Variety

". . . the film catches the generous spirit of the show folk's desire to do their bit. There is something very poignant and very noble in the aspect of famous people giving of themselves, often in a spirit of humility, that parting youngsters may have a few, brief, happy hours."

New York Times

A SONG TO REMEMBER
(1945)

A Columbia Picture. Produced by Louis F. Edelman. Directed by Charles Vidor. Color by Technicolor. From the story by Ernst Marischka. Screenplay, Sidney Buchman. Art Directors, Lionel Banks and Van Nest Polglase. Musical Supervisor, Mario Silva. Musical Director, M. W. Stoloff. Cameraman, Tony Gaudio. Editor, Charles Nelson. Released: January, 1945. 113 minutes.

Cast

Professor Joseph Elsner: Paul Muni; *George Sand:* Merle Oberon; *Frederic Chopin:* Cornel Wilde; *Franz Liszt:* Stephen Bekassy; *Constantia:* Nina Foch; *Louis Pleyel:* George Coulouris; *Henri Dupont:* Sig Arno; *Kalbrenner:* Howard Freeman; *Alfred DeMusset:* George Macready; *Madame Mercier:* Claire Dubrey; *Monsieur Jollet:* Frank Puglia; *Madame Lambert:* Fern Emmett; *Isabelle Chopin:* Sybil Merritt; *Monsieur Chopin:* Ivan Triesault; *Madame Chopin:* Fay Helm; *Isabelle Chopin (age 9):* Dawn Bender; *Chopin (age 10):* Maurice Tauzin; *Paganini:* Roxy Roth; *Balzac:* Peter Cusanelli; *Titus:* William Challee; *Jan:* William Richardson; *Postman:* Charles LaTorre; *Albert:* Earl Easton. *Also:* Gregory Gaye, Walter Bonn, Henry Sharp, Zoia Karabanova, Michael Visaroff, John George, Ian Wolfe, Norma Drury, Eugene Borden, and Al Luttringer.

The Film

In his first and only Technicolor picture, Muni played Professor Joseph Elsner, teacher of Frederic Chopin. Elsner, a well-known composer in his own right, is best remembered for his "Sabat Mater."

The narrative follows the career of Chopin (Cornel Wilde), beginning in Poland, where he and Elsner are members of a revolutionary organization determined to drive out the Russian government, which rules the country. While giving a private concert, Chopin insults a high-ranking Russian official by refusing to play for him. Both he and Elsner flee the country and go to Paris. There, the professor hopes to get his prize pupil recognition. Franz Liszt (Stephen Bekassy) immediately perceives Chopin's genius and, with the help of novelist George Sand (Merle Oberon), arranges for Louis Pleyel (George Coulouris) to manage him, as well as publish his music.

A Song to Remember. Players, Muni, Cornel Wilde, and Stephen Bekassy.

A Song to Remember. With Merle Oberon.

Chopin goes with George Sand, a selfish, domineering woman, to her country house for a short holiday, which, because of a strong romantic attachment between the two, develops into an indefinite stay. While living with George, Chopin writes many beautiful compositions, but ignores his most important, yet unfinished work, the "Polonaise," which captures the spirit of the people in his revolution-torn country.

Elsner receives a visit from Constantia (Nina Foch), a member of the Polish revolutionary organization, who informs the professor that some of the group's leaders have been imprisoned and money is needed to free them. Elsner visits Chopin and berates him for ignoring his true purpose in coming to Paris . . . to help the Polish people. Chopin has Pleyel arrange a concert tour for him with proceeds to go to the revolutionary group. Because he has chosen to go against her wishes in this instance, George Sand breaks off the relationship with her lover.

Chopin has a successful tour . . . playing the "Polonaise" at every engagement. However, his health fails and he dies, leaving his

A Song to Remember. With Claire Dubrey and Cornel Wilde.

A Song to Remember. Cornel Wilde, Stephen Bekassy, Merle Oberon, George Macready, Muni.

magnificent music for the world to enjoy.

The picture had two working titles during production, *The Song That Lived Forever* and *The Love of Madame Sand*.

Muni's role was actually a secondary one. Always a perfectionist in his portrayals, he had three pairs of special glasses ground by an oculist and encased in the steel rims prevalent to the period.

Cornel Wilde recalls the film: "I'd always admired Muni and greatly looked forward to working with him. I expected that such a dedicated actor would be helpful to a young performer, such as myself. I was in for a rude awakening.

"On the first day of shooting, I approached Muni and asked if, when he had time, we could read our key scenes over together, so we could each have an idea how the other was going to interpret their role. He looked at me for a minute, then stated, quite bluntly, 'Dear boy, I have done considerable research on Chopin and have my own interpretation as to how he should be portrayed. I will play to my conception . . . not yours.' "

Muni had many problems during this film and the strain shows on the screen. It's the most exaggerated and overblown performance of his film career. Just pure *ham*.

Glenn Ford was Muni's choice to play Chopin, but, with the war on, the young actor had chosen to enlist in the Marines instead. Muni may have resented Wilde's taking his friend's role and this would account for any hostility he exhibited toward him.

Also, Muni was unhappy that Columbia Pictures head, Harry Cohn, had barred Bella from the set, fearing that she might interfere with the director, as she had done on prior films. Director Charles Vidor, unfortunately, was unable to tone down Muni's performance.

Nina Foch recalls an incident during production: "It was Chopin's death scene. Everything kept going wrong. Lights blew out. Film got jammed in the camera. Finally, Muni became very upset and yelled, 'I can't turn this on and off like a faucet.' He was referring, of course, to his emotions. It was a great line and I sometimes use it when things get tense on a set because of technical problems."

Although Wilde received an Academy Award nomination for his role, none of the performances were distinguished. The highly fictionalized screenplay had few interesting moments. In fact, the only strong points of the picture were the elaborate sets and beautiful music.

A Song to Remember. With Stephen Bekassy.

What the Critics Said

"The dramatization of the life and times of Frederic Chopin, the Polish musician-patriot, is the most exciting presentation of an artist yet achieved by the screen.

". . . Paul Muni has a role much to his liking and his measure in the old music teacher, scolding and devoted, proud and disturbed by his pupil. Muni gives it a fine humor and a touching pathos."

Variety

". . . His characterization is amusing, even though fictional, but Mr. Muni too often plays without restraint. Apparently he didn't receive much direction from Charles Vidor."

New York Times

"This glorious picture is a major event in film history. It is one of the finest and most beautiful screen productions yet given to the world, and in the field of music films of its kind, it stands alone.

". . . Every performance in the film is outstanding. Paul Muni's delineation of the professor is one of the finest of his screen characterizations, brilliant in its delicate shadings. He lives the role, at times delightfully amusing, at others movingly powerful. His reading of the rebuke, which reawakens Chopin, is superfine."

Hollywood Reporter

COUNTER-ATTACK
(1945)

Presented by Columbia Pictures. Produced and Directed by Zoltan Korda. Screenplay by John Howard Lawson. Adapted from a play by Janet and Philip Stevenson, which was based upon a play by Ilya Vershinin and Mikhail Ruderman entitled *Pobyeda.* Photography, James Wong Howe. Art Direction, Stephen Goosson and Edward Jewell. Musical Score, Louis Gruenberg. Musical Director, M. W. Stoloff. Editor, Charles Nelson and Al Clark. Released: March, 1945. 83 minutes.

Cast

Alexei Kulkov: Paul Muni; *Lisa Elenko:* Marguerite Chapman; *Kirichenko:* Larry Parks; *Galkronye:* Philip Van Zandt; *Colonel Semenov:* George Macready; *Kostyuk:* Roman Bohnen; *Ernemann:* Harro Meller; *Vassilev:* Erik Rolf; *Stillman:* Rudolph Anders; *Mueller:* Ludwig Donath. *Also:* Ian Wolfe, Paul Andor, Frederick Giermann, Ivan Triesault, Louis Adlon, Trevor Bardette, and Richard Hale.

The Film

In 1945, Russia and the United States were allies, so it was not surprising that Columbia Pictures would make a film dealing with the plight of the Russian soldier. Hollywood had already done pictures on the Russian role in the war (such as *The North Star*), therefore the idea of having a Soviet hero was nothing new.

Muni played Alexei Kulkov, a simple Russian soldier, trapped in a bombed-out cellar during a raid on a German-held town. With him is a Russian girl, Lisa Elenko (Marguerite Chapman), and a group of German soldiers. The two Russians are outnumbered, but manage to hold the seven Germans at bay, not knowing which army will eventually rescue them.

Kulkov discovers that one of the Germans, Ernemann (Harro Meller), is an officer and the pair engage in a strange battle of wits, whereby they trade secret information on their respective armies. Kulkov reasons that, should the Germans dig them out, he can always kill Ernemann before he can pass on the information that the Soviet army is building an underwater bridge in order to facilitate the crossing of a strategic river.

Counter-Attack. Muni, Marguerite Chapman, Ludwig Donath, Philip Van Zandt, Frederick Giermann, and Rudolph Anders.

Counter-Attack. With Marguerite Chapman.

The hours drag on and both Kulkov and Lisa need their sleep. At one point, the Germans get control of a weapon and, before they are thwarted, Lisa is wounded. One of the Germans, Stillman (Rudolph Anders), is disillusioned with Hitler and the Nazi movement. He offers to keep his former comrades covered with a rifle, while Kulkov gets some sleep. The Russian gives him a weapon, but does not tell him it is not loaded. Stillman proves that he is loyal to the Allied cause by keeping the other Germans at bay.

Somebody begins digging into the cellar. Ernemann, believing it to be Germans, starts to shout the information he has obtained from Kulkov. The Russian shoots him.

The rescuers are the Russians, who have crossed the river and taken the town. After his prisoners are in custody, Kulkov is carried out on a stretcher . . . sound asleep.

During the shooting of the picture, the title was changed to *One Against Seven,* then, later, back to *Counter-Attack*.

A few years after the film's release, Muni's co-star, Larry Parks, Sidney Buchman, who was supervising for the studio, and writer

Counter-Attack. With Ludwig Donath.

Counter-Attack. With Larry Parks.

John Howard Lawson were named by the Un-American Activities Committee as having had Communist affiliations, with Lawson being one of the "infamous" Hollywood Ten. All three were, subsequently, blacklisted by the motion picture industry.

Although some critics thought its action too confined, the picture, adapted from a play by Janet and Philip Stevenson, which was based upon a play by Ilya Vershinin and Mikhail Ruderman entitled *Pobyeda,* garnered, for the most part, good reviews, with Muni giving an interesting performance. Unfortunately, it did not draw a large audience, which served to confirm the suspicions of many producers around Hollywood that the public was not interested in "buying" Paul Muni.

What the Critics Said

"Paul Muni, as Kulkov, turns in a superb performance in a difficult role."

Variety

"Zoltan Korda, whose *Sahara* remains one of the finer war pictures to issue from Hollywood, has performed an equally arresting job in *Counter-Attack,* a taut, dynamic screen drama, demonstrating that clever resourceful craftsmanship can combine entertainment and informative elements.

"Here is no slipshod demonstration of phoney war heroics, but a cannily constructed, excellently knit screenplay that shrewdly fastens its action on a single incident in the Soviet march back over the territory occupied by the Germans early in the war.

". . . Paul Muni creates a forceful characterization of the grim, determined Soviet soldier—a performance notable for its restraint and sharp simplicity."

Hollywood Reporter

"Well written and well directed within the limits of one room, the picture still owes its fascination to the performers in the leading roles. Mr. Muni gives a fine representation of the Russian with a stubborn clever mind, and drops in just sufficient Slavic clowning to keep the role from going monotonous and dull."

New York Times

Counter-Attack. With Marguerite Chapman and Rudolph Anders.

"Paul Muni gives one of those thoughtful characterizations of the Red Army paratrooper, which is too studied and repetitive for comfort even when he is wielding a tommy-gun."

New York Herald-Tribune

ANGEL ON MY SHOULDER
(1946)

A United Artists Release of a Charles R. Rogers Production. Directed by Archie Mayo. Original Story by Harry Segall. Screenplay by Harry Segall and Roland Kibbee. Music Composed and Directed by Dimitri Tiomkin. Associate Producer, David W. Siegel. Cinematography, James Van Trees. Editorial Supervisor, George Arthur. Film Editor, Asa Clark. Art Director, Bernard Herzbrun. Sound, Frank Webster. Special Effects, Harry Redmond, Jr. Photographic Effects, Howard Anderson. Released: September, 1946. 95 minutes.

Cast

Eddie Kagle: Paul Muni; *Barbara Foster:* Anne Baxter; *Nick:* Claude Rains; *Dr. Higgins:* Onslow Stevens; *Albert:* George Cleveland; *Smiley:* Hardie Albright; *Bellamy:* James Flavin; *Minister:* Erskine Sanford; *Mrs. Bentley:* Marion Martin; *Chairman:* Jonathan Hale; *Jim:* Murray Alper; *Brazen Girl:* Joan Blair; *Scientist:* Fritz Leiber; *Warden:* Kurt Katch. *Also:* Sarah Padden, Addison Richards, Ben Welden, George Meeker, Lee Shumway, Russ Whiteman, James Dundee, Mike Lally, Saul Gorss, Duke Taylor, Edward Keane, and Chester Clute.

The Film

The Harry Segall/Roland Kibbee fantasy was both Muni's second gangster and second comedy film. Unfortunately, it suffered from comparison with Segall's earlier picture, *Here Comes Mr. Jordan,* which starred Robert Montgomery.

Muni played Eddie Kagle, a murdered gangster, who makes a pact with the Devil (Claude Rains), known in the film as Nick. Nick agrees to help Kagle get Smiley (Hardie Albright), the hood that shot him. In return, Eddie will take over the body and dishonor the name of an honest reform judge, whose accomplishments have reduced the number of "lost souls" that have journeyed to Hell recently.

After Kagle takes over, the judge's associates are disturbed by his unusual behavior and manner of speech. But Nick's attempts to discredit the jurist continually fail, as Eddie's primitive instincts cause him to react in ways that can only bring him praise. Inadvertently, he makes the judge a hero.

Angel on My Shoulder. With Joan Blair and Fritz Leiber.

Eddie also falls in love with the judge's fiancée, Barbara (Anne Baxter) and decides to change his ways when a minister's sermon makes him realize that the Devil cannot harm him if he does only good.

Smiley is killed when he accidentally falls from a window. Nick argues with Kagle that he must return to Hell with him, so that the judge can marry Barbara. Eddie sees the logic of this, realizing that if *he* stays on Earth, he will be depriving the judge of the remainder of his natural life.

As they depart for Hades, however, Eddie blackmails Nick with the threat that he will embarrass him by telling his disciples that he, Nick, almost lost one of his "souls." Desperate, Nick agrees to leave the judge alone and to make Eddie a trustee in Hell.

Anne Baxter recalls that Muni seemed very insecure during the making of *Angel on My Shoulder:* "I think he was trying to recapture *Scarface.* His career was in a downward slide and he wanted the film to be more than it was.

"Archie Mayo was not a director in depth, which, of course, was an approach completely in contrast to Muni, who had to know the

Angel on My Shoulder. With Claude Rains.

Angel on My Shoulder. With Anne Baxter.

meaning behind every syllable. The two were in constant conflict, which made for a very unhappy set."

The tranquillity of the cast and crew was further marred when, at the end-of-production party, a grip accidently fell from a catwalk to his death.

Although the picture did nothing to further Muni's career, it did have some entertaining scenes, particularly the ones between Kagle and Nick. At one point, the uneducated Eddie decides that he's had enough of his companion from Hell, yet the worse thing he can think to call him is a "Bee-zell-bub!"

Viewing both films today, *Angel* holds up better than *Here Comes Mr. Jordan,* probably because Muni is a more interesting actor to watch than Montgomery. Rains, incidently, played the title role (or "God") in the earlier picture.

What the Critics Said

"Muni turns in a new type of characterization and does a bang-up

Angel on My Shoulder. With Anne Baxter.

Angel on My Shoulder. With Claude Rains and Anne Baxter.

job with it, gradual transition in his character being fine example of acting."

Variety

"If author Harry Segall had written this picture first, before he wrote *Here Comes Mr. Jordan,* it might be hailed as a novel fantasy. For the story of *Angel On My Shoulder,* while full of hokum, is pretty good. . . .

". . . As we say, this might all seem quite novel and intriguing if it were not that Mr. Segall . . . and Mr. Jordan—had been over this ground before. Mr. Muni's performance of the gangster is aggressive and versatile, even though he does sometimes make the character look and act like the monster of Frankenstein. . . .

". . . But the story is so imitative—and is repeated so dutifully —that it's hard to feel any more towards it than a mildly nostalgic regard."

New York Times

STRANGER ON THE PROWL
(1953)

A Generaleine Release of a Riviera-Tirreni (Adolfo Baiocchi) Production. Directed by Andrea Forzano (Joseph Losey). Screenplay by Ben Barzman from a story by Nissim Calef. Camera, Henri Alekan. Music, G. C. Sonzogno. Editor, Thelma Connell. Italian title: *Imbarco a Mezzanotte*. Original title: *Encounter*. Released November, 1953. 87 minutes.

Cast

The Man: Paul Muni; *Mrs. Fontana:* Luisa Rossi; *Angela:* Joan Lorring; *Giacomo:* Vittorio Manunta; *Peroni:* Aldo Silvani; *Inspector:* Arnoldo Foa; *Castelli:* Alfredo Varelli.

The Film

Stranger on the Prowl was Muni's only film to be shot in a European country. He did not enjoy working in Italy and the entire experience was an unhappy one for him.

The picture was initially called *Encounter* and had an original length of 180 minutes. Unfortunately, by the time it opened in the United States, the running time had been shortened to 87 minutes.

Muni, referred to in the cast list only as "The Man," was a desperate vagrant, attempting to sell his revolver in order to raise money for an illegal passage on a freighter. Finding little success, he steals some cheese from a dairy shop and, in an attempt to stop the owner from screaming for help, accidentally strangles her.

The crime is witnessed by a young boy, Giacomo (Vittorio Manunta). He filches milk from the shop and decides to flee with The Man.

The pair are sheltered for a time by Angela (Joan Lorring), a maid in a wealthy household. She has a brief romantic interlude with the murderer, who has been wounded by the authorities.

The Man is eventually cornered by the police and killed. Giacomo is reunited with his laundress mother (Luisa Rossi).

The picture was directed by Joseph Losey, however, because of problems he was having with the Un-American Activities Committee at the time, the pseudonym of Andrea Forzano was used in order to facilitate the film's release in the United States through United Artists.

Stranger on the Prowl. With Alfred Varelli.

Stranger on the Prowl.

Stranger on the Prowl.

Although critics around the country expressed pleasure that Muni was back on the screen after an absence of seven years, the picture received only mild reviews and did little business. Perhaps, had Losey been able to edit the film as he had wanted, the final result would have been much better.

What the Critics Said

"Downbeat, weighty story will hold picture's English version to spotty returns in U.S. secondary situations, although the Paul Muni name may help.

". . . this picture has its suspenseful moments and unfolds in a satisfying manner. Muni's experience carries the vehicle. . . ."

Variety

"*Stranger on the Prowl* is a beautifully acted drama with good

Stranger on the Prowl. With Vittorio Manunta.

Stranger on the Prowl. With Leon Lenoir and players.

exploitation potential in Paul Muni's return to the screen after much too long an absence.

"Muni punches over all the fear, anger and misery of a hunted man, who realizes his time is up but despairingly cries out against the injustice of being cut down in what he feels is his prime."

Hollywood Reporter

"Since the absence of Paul Muni from the screen is to be deplored, the fact that he once again is appearing in a film should come as good news.

"But his return to the movies in *Stranger on the Prowl* . . . is something less than an important event. For this melodrama, filmed in Italy with a predominantly native cast (which speaks English) is, despite some philosophical innuendoes, a manhunt pure and simple. With the help of some solid portrayals, *Stranger on the Prowl* moves fairly swiftly against the authentic backgrounds of Pisa and Leghorn, but it is merely surface drama that is generally being enacted.

". . . Although he is hampered by a script that does not afford him much latitude, Mr. Muni endows the role of the fugitive with strength, if not stature. He is an unlettered man, but one who is not insensitive to the accumulated injustices that place him in an untenable position."

New York Times

THE LAST ANGRY MAN
(1959)

A Columbia Picture. Produced by Fred Kohlmar. Directed by Daniel Mann. Screenplay by Gerald Green from his novel of the same name. Adaptation, Richard Murphy. Music composed by George Duning. Music Conducted by Morris Stoloff. Cinematography, James Wong Howe. Art Director, Carl Anderson. Editor, Charles Nelson. Gowns, Jean Louis. Sound, Harry Mills. Released: October, 1959. 93 minutes.

Cast

Dr. Sam Abelman: Paul Muni; *Woodrow Wilson Thrasher:* David Wayne; *Anne Thrasher:* Betsy Palmer; *Dr. Max Vogel:* Luther Adler; *Myron Malkin:* Joby Baker; *Alice Taggart:* Joanna Moore; *Sarah Abelman:* Nancy R. Pollock; *Josh Quincy:* Billy Dee Williams; *Mrs. Quincy:* Claudia McNeil; *Lyman Gattling:* Robert F. Simon; *Ben Loomer:* Dan Tobin; *Nobody Home:* Godfrey Cambridge; *Miss Bannaham:* Helen Chapman; *Girl Left on Porch:* Cicely Tyson.

The Film

When Muni agreed to return to Hollywood for his first picture in thirteen years, it was with the basic understanding that *he* would "run the show." He'd taken five months to decide whether he would do the film in the first place. In fact, Columbia Pictures head, Harry Cohn, had already given up hope of securing Muni's services and had begun negotiating with Peter Ustinov to star in the film version of Gerald Green's novel.

Prior to the start of production, Muni demanded that certain changes be made in the script and both producer Fred Kohlmar and director Daniel Mann agreed to them. But when it came time to film these scenes and they had not been rewritten, the actor refused to go before the cameras until all promises were kept. Ultimately, the project ran several weeks over schedule.

In his final film, Muni was Dr. Sam Abelman, an idealistic physician, who has lived and worked in a Brooklyn slum for forty-five years. Residing with him are his wife, Sarah (Nancy R. Pollock), and nephew, Myron Malkin (Joby Baker), an aspiring journalist.

Television producer Woodrow Wilson Thrasher (David Wayne)

The Last Angry Man. With David Wayne.

The Last Angry Man. With Nancy R. Pollock and Joby Baker.

reads a newspaper article, written by Myron, about Abelman's work in the ghetto. He sells the idea to his boss, Ben Loomer (Dan Tobin), that the doctor would be an excellent subject for a new show to be sponsored by a drug company.

Abelman is not interested in doing the program. But Thrasher promises Myron a job with the television station if the ambitious young man will help him to change his uncle's mind. Myron puts the producer in touch with Dr. Max Vogel (Luther Adler). The Park Avenue specialist had gone to medical school with Abelman and is his best friend. On Thrasher's promise that he will have the sponsor buy Abelman a home in a good neighborhood, Vogel agrees to help. He convinces his old friend that the show will give him the opportunity to speak his mind about the hypocrisy in the medical profession.

Abelman has taken a strong interest in Josh Quincy (Billy Dee Williams), a local tough. The doctor suspects that the youth has a possible brain tumor. Josh, however, refuses help and the elderly physician is always "chasing" him in order to administer treatment.

On the night of the live television show, Josh is arrested and Abelman goes to the local police station to see him. While there, he suffers a heart attack, which proves to be fatal. Vogel and Thrasher, as well as the ghetto community, realize that a great man has died.

The Last Angry Man was filmed on location in New York City, with interiors being shot in Hollywood.

Columbia originally assigned contract player Glenn Ford to play Thrasher, but, on the advice of Muni, who thought his friend should not accept a secondary role, he refused and David Wayne was hired.

Luther Adler, a friend of Muni's since *We Americans,* recalls the production: "On the first day of filming, I was in Muni's dressing room when he called in Danny Mann. Muni wanted something clarified in a particular scene and, as was his way, he took the entire morning to explain what he wanted. Finally, realizing that half a day was lost, Mann asked Muni to sum up what he wanted him to do with the scene. Muni's eyes lit up and he said, 'Ah! The scene must be *filtered, sifted, refined* and *distilled.*'

"When he left the dressing room, Dan turned to me and said, 'What does he think we're making . . . matzoh balls?' "

Billy Dee Williams, making his film debut, also reflects on Muni: "He was very kind to me and I came to regard him almost as a second grandfather. When we were rehearsing the hand-wrestling scene, I really tried to beat him. Actually, he's suppose to 'take' *me.*

He stopped the action and said, 'I'm not as young as I use to be.' Then he showed me how to fake it and the scene went quite well."

Although Muni, Adler, and Williams were highly praised by the press, the production itself was not. It was a very uneven picture, which just seemed to skim the surface of the Green novel. Box office was virtually nil.

Muni received his fifth Academy Award nomination for his performance.

What the Critics Said

"Paul Muni, who made some of the greatest pictures in history . . . has come back, with his remarkable powers undiminished, to score another great triumph in *The Last Angry Man.*"

Hollywood Reporter

"*The Last Angry Man* is a film as pungent and indelible as Brooklyn on a hot summer afternoon. It has faults; it does not live up to all its early promises, and, technically, it is sometimes patchy and uneven. But it is possible to overlook whatever imperfections stud

The Last Angry Man. With Billy Dee Williams and Claudia McNeil.

The Last Angry Man. With Billy Dee Williams.

The Last Angry Man.

The Last Angry Man. With Luther Adler.

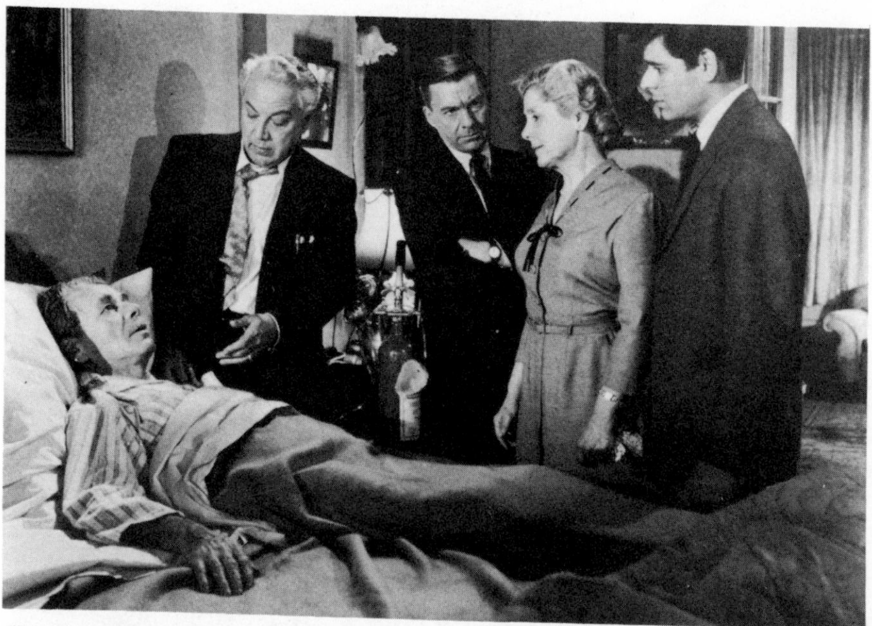

The Last Angry Man. Muni, Luther Adler, David Wayne, Nancy R. Pollock, and Joby Baker.

Fred Kohlmar's Columbia production because so much of it is so good and so rare.

"... Muni gives a superlative performance. Someone chides him at one point for thinking of himself as an Albert Schweitzer. A Schweitzer he isn't, but in Muni's character delineation it's apparent it's the men like him who keep the world going. Muni's acting is both old-time European grand-scale, and as anything by today's youngsters."

Variety

"Much of its moving appeal comes from a canny performance by Paul Muni in the leading role. Mr. Muni is a skillful old-timer who knows all the bold and subtle ways of bringing an interesting, robust character to glowing theatrical life.

"He knows how to blend the touching qualities of pathos and dignity in an old man, to cock his head and peer over his glasses with the arresting authority of a sage. He knows how to mumble little phrases that deceptively do justice to the man and thunder the grand, honest speeches that support a philosophy.

"Mr. Muni can illustrate a lifetime of self-reliance by pulling an old woolen muffler about his neck; he can pack mammoth scorn of petty creatures in the one expectorated word, 'Galoot!'

"That's why the somewhat hackneyed drama that Richard Murphy has compressed from Mr. Green's book seems a good deal more genuine and arresting than it really is. For the drama itself displays the good man in only a few obvious charitable deeds, and it equates against him the conventional insincerity of television commerce in ridiculously broad and virtually artificial terms."

New York Times

Paul Muni
September 22, 1895–August 25, 1967.